Go to the Land of Moriah

Kathy Stewart

© Kathy Stewart 2020

Freedom Publishing Limited
12 Dukes Court. Bognor Road
Chichester, PO19 8FX, United Kingdom
www.freedompublishing.net

ISBN: 978-1-908154-51-4

British Library Cataloguing in Publication Data. A catalogue record for this book is available from the British Library

Cover by Esther Kotecha, EKDesign
Typesetting by Avocet Typeset, Bideford, Devon, EX39 2BP
Printed in the UK

Dedication

This book is dedicated to the Lord Jesus Christ

*"For from Him and through Him and to Him
are all things.*

To Him be the Glory forever! Amen"
(Romans 11:36)

Thank you for the adventure!

Endorsement

"This is an incredible book, written by an ordinary but amazing couple who obeyed the call of God upon their lives and in so doing transformed the lives of many others.

I thoroughly recommend it, if only for the testimony to the Lord's keeping power of His people Israel. But it is much more than that as you will see as you walk with them through one seemingly impossible situation to another."

Beryl Moore, Oasis Community Trust

Table of Contents

Foreword   7
Preface   9
1   "Go to the land of Moriah"   11
2   My Christian Beginnings   19
3   Early days   27
4   The Birth   31
5   The Biblical Significance of Mount Moriah   35
6   God's Teaching About Israel   41
7   The God of the Unexpected   45
8   Obedience   51
9   Cleansing   55
10   Divine Disciplines   61
11   Our different roles   71
12   God chooses the workers   75
13   Sharing our material blessings   83
14   God's Exhortation to help those in need   89
15   Mount Moriah Trust 2002 – 2005   91
16   Mount Moriah Trust 2006 – 2009   113
17   Mount Moriah Trust 2010 – 2013   125
18   Mount Moriah Trust 2014 – 2017   151
19   Mount Moriah Trust 2018 – 2020   167
20   God's Appointed Times   175
21   The Supporters   179
22   A Ministry of Encouragement   191
23   Prejudice   195
24   Greater Outreach: Teaching from the Word of God   197
25   The Roots go deep   203
26   The Lord's work continues   207
27   Pastors' Testimonies   211
28   Supporters' Testimonies   243
29   Join the Lord in His work   255

Acknowledgements

My grateful thanks go to:

My husband Tony, a tower of strength, my faithful friend and co-worker in everything. He has worked so hard to help me put this book together;

The Pastors and Leaders that we partner with in Israel, Gaza and the West Bank for their contributions to the book;

Mount Moriah Trust supporters: Pastor John Angliss, Sally Williams, Tony & Sally Tester, Brian & Brenda Baldwin, Nethanel & Tabitha Lam, Gwenda Kuo, Wayne & Pauline Perry for their contributions to the book;

Beryl Moore and Joyce McIntyre to whom I owe so much and for reading and appraising the draft manuscript;

Mark Dunman Mount Moriah Trustee for proof reading and appraising the draft manuscript;

Sally Williams, friend and Mount Moriah Trustee who kindly typed the first draft – such a blessing.

Praise and thanks to God for each and every one of you. By His Grace the work goes on.

Foreword

I feel very privileged to be asked to write the foreword to this splendid book. I and my wife Margaret have known Tony and Kathy Stewart since 2006 when we were introduced by Ken Burnett. I have led a weekly prayer group for Israel over many years in our home town, and I had discussed with Ken how we could support Messianic fellowships financially in Israel. He said that The Mount Moriah Trust (MMT) was just the vehicle and thus began our long and fruitful co-operation with Tony and Kathy.

As the reader will discover, MMT is almost unique in using none of the gift money towards expenses. Tony and Kathy, their trustees and other helpers cover their own travelling and administration costs. It is a real bonus to the giver to know that every pound they donate goes to needy believers in Israel. For many years now these believers have included Arab Christians in Israel, the West Bank and Gaza as well as Messianic Jews in Israel.

This is a ministry that has been led by the Holy Spirit from the start. The reader will learn how Tony and Kathy were led by the Lord to set up the ministry and how they sought the Lord for His guidance at every stage. Along the way God taught them many lessons: obedience, waiting for God's guidance and timing, and faith in His promises. Perhaps the biggest lesson was the instruction to trust God for the financial provision – they could publicise the work of the Trust, but they were never to ask for money.

This has proved particularly testing when God, from time to time, appeared to withhold the funds, wanting the recipients to trust and look to Him rather than MMT.

As the reader journeys through this book they will meet many interesting and dedicated people: pastors, wives and their families, needy recipients and their families and people who have felt led to support the work of MMT. One cannot but help be affected by the hardship so many believers and ordinary citizens suffer. Many Christians who support Israel, see it as an advanced nation at the cutting edge of technology in medicine and industry, and are not aware of the divide between rich and poor and the lack of a safety net for many citizens.

This is where charities such as MMT come into play. They help to plug this poverty gap in the very specific area of Christian need. It is a sad fact that certain Jewish groups seek to persecute Messianic believers in Jesus, causing them hardship, because they believe they are no longer Jews! If this leads to the breadwinner losing his job, food parcels and other support will tide the family over such difficult times.

The reader will learn of the fascinating journey through which the Lord has led Tony and Kathy. I pray that the reader will enjoy the journey and be inspired to do exploits for God in the way that He has used this very humble couple.

Mark Dunman
(author: *Has God really finished with Israel?* and *The Return of Jesus Christ*)

Preface

This book is Testimony to the Goodness and Loving-kindness of God to all He has made. In everything, we see His Hand, His purposes and plans that He has accomplished and will continue to fulfil for His Glory and Honour.

We stand in awe of His vastness, His immensity, His Sovereignty and His Almighty Power and Authority.

As you read this book, marvel at Who God is. He is at the centre of **all** things. He has worked throughout history and continues to perform His Mighty deeds to accomplish all that He has planned.

He chooses whom He chooses to fulfil His will. A life surrendered to God can be His channel for His eternal purposes.

Read how He chose two ordinary people to bring about His extraordinary work – The Mount Moriah Trust.

It is a story of His Heart of Love for His ancient Covenant people, the believing Jews and the Christian Arabs in Israel, Gaza and the West Bank.

It is a story of His transforming Grace and transforming Love in the lives of those He calls.

Be inspired by Almighty God, the Creator of Heaven and Earth, the Eternal, Everlasting, Unchanging One, the Great I AM, the Coming King.

We give Him all the Praise and Thanksgiving as we see His Almighty Power at work and His absolute Sovereignty over all that happens, both now and for evermore.

We are humbled to see the Greatness of our God and we bow in reverent worship of the Great I AM.

To God be the Glory.

This book has been written to show how God knows everything about us. He knew us before time began. Our lives are planned – no detail too small, no circumstance too large. He knows, sees and plans everything. He weaves together the past, the present and the future. He is working, the Master Craftsman, on the tapestry of our lives. He is looking at the picture He is making. We only see the messy underside, the knots, the loose ends, the straggly threads. Everything in our lives is included in that picture, the good and the bad. In His Hands everything is woven into the work of art He is creating, giving depth and breadth, highs and lows, peaks and troughs, perspective and dimension.

Each one of us is His workmanship, a beautiful tapestry in the making.

For we are God's masterpiece. Ephesians 2:10 (NLT)

Chapter 1

"Go to the land of Moriah"
Genesis 22:2 (NKJV)

*"I want you to begin a Trust to help needy believers in
the land of Israel. You are to call it the Mount Moriah Trust.
I AM birthing the work."*

These were the Words of the Lord, spoken into my spirit in August
2001.

I had returned in May from Jerusalem after attending a David
Hathaway Conference, 'Fire over Jerusalem'. At the time I didn't know
anything about David Hathaway and his ministry, but I had received
information about the Conference in the post and felt prompted in
my spirit to go. It was not easy to arrange because my elderly father
was living with us and it meant that Tony, my husband and I had to
find a care home for him for a week. But the pull to go was strong and
everything fell into place.

The 2nd Intifada (Uprising) had begun in September 2000 and Israel
was suffering from the effects of suicide bombers, killing themselves
and as many Israelis as possible. Jerusalem was particularly targeted.
Bus bombs and restaurant bombs were increasingly becoming
the way of life for Israelis. Tourists stayed away and Jerusalem was
deserted. Israelis were stoically getting on with their lives despite the
horrendous dangers, but Jerusalem was suffering from the absence of
tourists.

In David Hathaway's letter from Eurovision written a month

before the Conference, he asked for much prayer for the work and the difficulties in Israel:

"Since we received the challenge from the Lord for Israel, we have been under satanic attack. The constant tension in Israel and the desire to evangelise in Jerusalem needs your urgent prayers. Even Jesus wept over Jerusalem 2,000 years ago. It is reputedly the hardest place to evangelise and especially to see miracles of healing, but I know that God loves His people and wants to gather them into His Kingdom. War clouds are gathering in Israel, they are preparing for an attack. Saddam Hussein has reputedly called up an army of 6–7 million and is training them. Most of the Arab nations will support the alliance between Iraq, Syria and the PLO. Only Egypt and Jordan are seeking moderation. That is why we must be in Jerusalem now!

I have been so burdened lately and felt a new urgency to pray, there has been a heaviness on me, the answer is the challenge of Israel. Never in 4,000 years has Israel faced such a threat as she does today. Yet in the past God always raised up a Moses, an Elijah, a David and a Messiah! We sing 'These are the days of Elijah' – Israel needs an Elijah, or rather a Messiah today!"

The Conference was held at the Jerusalem International Conference Centre (JICC), next door to the Crowne Plaza Hotel where I stayed. The Conference Centre was targeted by Yad L'achim, the anti-missionary haredi organisation, Jerusalem City Council members and haredi Members of the Knesset (MKs), the Israeli Parliament. Around the Conference Centre audio tapes, scrunched and tangled, had been placed as a means of cursing the meetings and those taking part. David Hathaway led us in a search to find these demonic symbols and pray over the building and the Conference.

Letters were left by Yad L'achim around the Conference Centre saying:

Dear Christian Visitor,

Welcome to Jerusalem. We wish you a joyous encounter with the land, people and tradition of Israel. But we would like to point out that this blessing is conditional upon refraining from <u>any</u> activity, which could, in any way, be construed as missionary in purpose.

Jews have come to Israel from all over the world in order to be free from both physical and spiritual persecution. Jews see conversion to another faith (and we consider Christianity as such, whatever the opinion of well-meaning Christians may be) as a spiritual form of genocide! The people decimated by the Holocaust will strongly oppose any attempt to proselytize us.

Although, as a believer, you may be accustomed to share the message of your faith with everyone you meet, such activity is viewed as hostile by Jewish tradition. The results of such activity could lead to a major public outcry. The watchful eyes of the Jewish nation are upon you!

If your intention is to be a real friend of Israel, we welcome it, as our tradition has great respect for the righteous of the nations. But a true friend approaches his friend's deepest inner beliefs with modesty, humility, and respect. G-d gave us the Torah 3,500 years ago at Sinai and we humbly suggest that our understanding of it is <u>at least</u> as good as yours! In the light of all the above, hopefully you understand why missions to Jews in Israel and in the rest of the world should be avoided and opposed.

We trust that you will receive this message in the spirit of peace in which it is being given.

Yad L'achim

P.O. Box 5195 Jerusalem 91051

In an article in the Jerusalem Post after the event it was reported:

> The Conference called 'Fire over Jerusalem: Celebration of the
> God of Israel', and featuring international evangelist David
> Hathaway as well as foreign and local believers in Jesus, went
> ahead as scheduled despite protests by Yad L'achim, Jerusalem
> City Council members and haredi MKs. The missionaries'
> insistence and the capitulation of the Israeli authorities, which
> allowed these missionaries to act freely and to entice innocent
> Jewish souls under the guise of healing, is truly shocking",
> said Yad L'achim's Alex Artousky.

During the Conference, I met Moshe, a taxi driver based at the hotel,
a Messianic Jewish believer who drove a few of us around Jerusalem
one afternoon, explaining the impact of the Intifada on daily living
– hotels, restaurants, taxis, businesses, the airline – were all suffering
because there were no tourists. This had a knock-on effect on the
whole economy.

I began to realise that the Lord was showing me His heart for His
land and people and the needs of His Jewish people at this difficult
time.

After the Conference, I stayed on for a few days to look around the
sights of Jerusalem. Moshe arranged for me to visit the Western Wall
Tunnels with a specialist guide – an amazing underground excavation
at the site of Solomon's Temple on Mount Moriah. It is a very special
place as described in the guidebook:

> "Here is a realm rich in roots – here Abraham was warned not
> to 'lift your hand against the youth (Isaac).'
> Here one can imagine the songs and the music of the
> Levites. The stories evoke memories of King David and
> Solomon, of Ezra and Nehemiah, of the Maccabees and the
> Sages. Kings and prophets walked along these paths.
> Here at the foot of the Western Wall, more than any other

place on earth, the memories of Jewish past mingle with the hopes of Jewish future."

At one point on the tour I felt the Presence of the Lord, a powerful Presence that left me feeling weak and powerless. I had never felt anything like that before. The guide was saying that we were close to the area of the Holy of Holies.

I felt so overwhelmed by the experience that I had to say to Moshe that I couldn't continue with the rest of the morning's tour we had planned. He understood and took me back to the hotel, where I spent the rest of the day in quiet contemplation of the Lord's Glorious Power and Glory. I wasn't sure what it all meant, but I was deeply moved in my innermost being.

On the flight home, the Lord said *"Help this man Moshe."* I said "Lord, You will have to make this right with my husband, Tony. He will wonder who I have met and why we should help him."

But the Lord had already worked on Tony's heart and he readily agreed we should help Moshe and his family during this difficult time.

We really didn't understand at the time the significance of what the Lord was asking us to do. He was testing us to see if we would obey His commands. Would we enter into His heart of love for His people? We didn't realise that this was going to be our work in the future – *"to help needy believers in Israel."* As He bonded us with Moshe and his family, He was giving us the blueprint for the Trust.

Obedience to His commands is so vital to the Lord, even when we don't understand what He is doing or the significance of what He asks. Obedience brings blessing:

If you fully obey the Lord your God and carefully follow all His commands... all these blessings will come upon you and accompany you if you obey the Lord your God. Deuteronomy 28:1-2 .[Emphasis added]

15

How precious it is to share in the Lord's heart of love for His people! Three months later in August 2001 during my Quiet Time with the Lord, I received His call to begin the Mount Moriah Trust.

> *"I want you to begin a Trust to help needy believers in the land of Israel. You are to call it the Mount Moriah Trust. I AM birthing the work."*

When He said He was birthing the work I understood that the Trust would come into being as a charity nine months later in May 2002.

It was interesting that I was 'between' churches at the time of God's calling. The Lord told me to leave the Kerith Centre Church in Bracknell. I loved being there but they believed that God has finished with Israel. He said that it was time to "go to a new place." I had heard that the South of Reading Christian Fellowship at Three Mile Cross had a heart for Israel and felt that this was where the Lord was leading me. This was where He wanted the Trust to be birthed. Pastor John Angliss was very encouraging and supportive and became one of the Trust's first Trustees.

Looking back, I believe that if I had not obeyed the Lord to move to the church of His choosing, the Trust would not have been born. He gives us free will choice, but to obey God is vital, otherwise we can miss out on the plans He has for us.

Before joining the Church at Three Mile Cross I went to visit Beryl, a faithful servant of the Lord who ran the Oasis Community Trust, to share the vision of the Lord. She was very encouraging and explained how she had begun the Trust, giving guidelines on how to go about establishing a charity. God chose who I was to speak to about the vision for the work. When you need to consult someone on an issue such as this it is so important to let God lead you to the right person.

Comments that I received later from very sincere Christians did question whether we should have joined an existing ministry working for Israel and the Jewish people rather than begin a new ministry.

But I knew that I knew that the Lord had given His command to begin the Mount Moriah Trust. It was important to be faithful to the vision that God had given, to be steadfast, to believe and obey what He said.

Tony was wonderful, so supportive and helpful. What a precious gift from the Lord he is! He began to look at how to go about setting up a trust/charity and all the paperwork that the Charity Commission would require.

But we needed to know what the charity would do and how it would operate. The Lord said, *"Go the land of Moriah and I will show you the next step."* We were both to go to Israel and there He would show us what He wanted us to do as a charity.

A prophecy had been given at the Conference in Jerusalem that Israel was in a time of lean years, which had begun in September 2000 when the troubles with the Palestinians began. We went to Israel in February 2002 when the Israelis were already eighteen months into this period of famine and the situation was getting worse. We wondered – would this work be for a season only?

In February 2002, Tony took a week's leave from work and we went to Jerusalem. Ken Burnett, founder of Prayer for Israel, and Pastor John Angliss had given us names and contact details of people in Israel who might be able to help us. We rang them, left messages asking them to call back, but got no replies. God closed every door and told us to *"be still."* We learned that God never says "stand still", "be still", or "wait" unless He is going to do something. We need to allow Him to work. At the very end of our week, just as we were preparing to leave, the Lord showed us through our talks with Moshe that He wanted us to help families who were struggling to cope. God's perfect timing!

The Lord said to us, *"The families will be 'in the natural'*, a channel for Him to operate *'in the supernatural'."* We were also to learn one of His abiding golden principles: God gives us a little and if we use His gifts well, He then gives us more. We were to give out what we had and then we would receive more.

See the 'Parable of the Talents' Matthew 25:14-30

In Jerusalem we were so blessed by the weather, the hotel, Moshe driving us around – the Lord's care of us in every way. There were only twenty guests staying in the large Crowne Plaza Hotel. Only one floor was open and meals were eaten in the foyer as the restaurant had been closed. Israelis were saying how blessed they were by our being there. They were amazed by our visit and asked if we were frightened and said they admired and respected us for coming – "Kol hakavod" they said, which means "All honour to you". It was truly a blessed time.

It was a special time to be the only Gentiles amongst Jews, especially at the dinners in the hotel. People said, "You must be the only tourists in Israel!" Certainly this seemed true in Jerusalem.

Through Moshe's Fellowship and the House Group he led, the Lord showed us three families who were in desperate need and we knew the work had begun! As our week came to an end, I prayed:

"Lord, I pray that You will continue to lead us to the next stage. I can hardly believe this is happening. What a privilege to serve You in this way, helping Your people in Your land. What an honour! Keep us close to You, Lord. Help us to serve You faithfully and not to be overwhelmed."

Together with the Lord, Tony and I had begun the work of the Mount Moriah Trust:

perfectly united in mind and thought. 1 Corinthians 1:10

Chapter 2

My Christian Beginnings

I know the plans I have for you declares the Lord.
Jeremiah 29:11

I gave my life to the Lord Jesus at a Youth Convention on the Isle of Wight when I was fifteen. I came home knowing that there was more to Christianity than just going now and again to church and paying lip service to God at certain times. It was about a relationship with Jesus Christ, a commitment, a way of living.

I bombarded my family – mum, dad, aunt, uncle and grandmother one afternoon with the Truth of Jesus. They sat stunned and silent wondering what was happening to me. My mum became worried that I was becoming a 'religious fanatic' and hurried to see the Headmistress who comforted her by saying – "Don't worry, it's her age, she's an impressionable teenager, she'll grow out of it."

Unfortunately, that is what happened. As I went to a Polytechnic College, then to Teacher Training College, I decided I wanted to experience 'life', to see what the world offered, to be free!

I had no idea then that there were two kingdoms – the Kingdom of Light and the Kingdom of Darkness, and that the world is at this time, under the rule of Satan since the Fall of mankind:

the whole world is under the control of the evil one. 1 John 5:19.

That ancient serpent called the devil, or Satan, who leads the whole world astray. Revelation 12:9.

Unknowingly, by walking away from Jesus, I had opted to live in the Kingdom of Darkness.

I embarked on a journey that eventually led me into the occult. I always seemed to meet strange people from strange cults and beliefs. Satan had a field day! For 33 years, to my shame, I went further away from the Lord.

But what an amazing, gracious, loving and persistent God He is.

Much later I realised that through all those years, God was sovereignly watching over, protecting, guiding me back to Him.

As with His treasured possession, His firstborn son, Israel, the nation had abandoned the Lord, their God, and fallen into idolatry and disobedience, as I had done. They had committed spiritual adultery, but yet in His compassion and Fatherly love, the God of Israel was watching over them.

> *Indeed, He who watches over Israel will neither slumber nor sleep.*
> *The Lord watches over you ....*
> *The Lord will keep you from all harm –*
> *He will watch over your life;*
> *the Lord will watch over your coming and going*
> *both now and for evermore.* Psalm 121:4–8

God had given me Tony, a loving, faithful husband, who like Father God Himself was always there for me – stable and protective. I did not realise it at the time, but Tony's love is a reflection of God's love.

The Lord brought me to a place where I questioned what life was about.

Tony and I had a very good life; stability, travel, a comfortable lifestyle, but I began to feel that something was missing. There was an emptiness inside me.

As I travelled with Tony on his business trips around the country, I found myself going into churches, sitting quietly, talking to God about how I felt, things that bothered me, problems with family issues.

Some months later at a friend's farewell get together before they went away as missionaries, Martin their son-in-law, a passionate believer in Jesus, approached me and said: "The Lord knows you have been seeking – open your heart and let Him in."

I was stunned. This young man hardly knew me, let alone know that I had been visiting churches and praying to God.

Even more amazing, as I looked at him, I saw in his eyes a Being looking at me with such love and understanding, such a penetrating gaze, an all-knowing gaze, that I never saw in his or anyone else's eyes again. I realised much later that it was the Holy Spirit and I have never forgotten that moment or that look.

Nevertheless, it took me fifteen months to act upon those words. I knew that this time there would be no turning back from the Lord. Would I be able to keep such a commitment? Would I be able to stand up for my faith in the face of opposition? I wanted to be sure I wouldn't back down again. Jesus tells us to count the cost of being a disciple. Luke 14:26-33.

It took a small family crisis which brought me to a low place before I made the decision to give my life to the Lord, this time for good. I went to see a Christian couple, Dave and Jean, who led me in prayer and repentance to Jesus. It was 1993, I was now 48 and on fire for the Lord, who had died for me and who had given me a second chance after all those years of my sin and rebellion.

Praise God, He is the God of the second, third, fourth, in fact many chances if we return to Him in repentance, seeking forgiveness.

I think of Peter who denied Jesus three times on the night of His crucifixion and the devastation he felt when he realised what he had done to His Lord. But the love of Jesus who, after His resurrection, re-instated Peter and commissioned him to be an Apostle, feeding and caring for His sheep and lambs. John 21:15–19.

I joined the Kerith Centre, a Holy Spirit filled church in Bracknell.

I was hungry for the Word of God, read the Bible, devoured Christian books, listened to teaching tapes, attended courses, conferences, joined a house group, and always answered altar calls at churches and gatherings for prayer. I would find myself prostrate on the floor before the Lord, ready to do His will, ready to be surrendered to Him.

One of the elders of the church, Mick Taylor, said to me one day: "you're on a marathon, not a sprint." He warned me of burnout if I continued at the rate I was going! I appreciated his concern. It is something we need to be aware of especially when we are new believers.

By God's grace, I did not suffer burnout. It was as the Lord had said in the beginning that He was working quickly through me. He had given me a hunger and thirst for Himself and His word, and the spiritual stamina to pursue Him.

I discovered Ellel Ministries and attended courses and conferences, becoming impacted by their Biblical teaching. I went on healing retreats and had personal ministry appointments, and with the help of counsellors, the Lord dealt with and set me free from all the adverse situations I had been in, all the occult involvements I had dabbled in. I had so much to repent of. Through Jesus and His precious blood shed for my sin, I was cleansed of all sin, guilt, fear and anxiety. I was being changed from the inside out.

I loved the Lord passionately and knew I was in His Kingdom now and for eternity. Nothing or no-one could take me out of it.

Jesus said:

> *I give them eternal life, and they shall never perish; no-one can snatch them out of My hand. My Father, who has given them to Me, is greater than all; no-one can snatch them out of My Father's hand. I and the Father are one.* John 10:28–30.

I knew the truth of the words from Colossians 1:13:

For He has rescued us from the dominion of darkness and brought us into the Kingdom of the Son He loves, in whom we have redemption, the forgiveness of sins.

My life, though 'full', had been in reality 'empty' without Him.

It was as Jesus said:

You do not realise that you are wretched, pitiful, poor, blind and naked. Revelation 3:17.

Francis Frangipane in his book "The Shelter of the Most High" says: "The truth is that in ourselves we are incomplete, but in Christ we have been made complete" (Colossians 2:10). Jesus fills that God-shaped hole in us that makes us whole.

What an incredible God, who had watched over me, protected me and given me a second chance, a choice to follow Him. I had been rescued from Satan's Kingdom, washed in Jesus's precious blood – ready to serve Him out of my deep love and gratitude for my Saviour and Lord.

When I met Martin again, the same young man who had spoken the words of the Lord to me, he said that "God was going to work quickly through me." The Lord gave the Scripture: "*I know the plans I have for you*", declares the Lord, "*plans to prosper you and not harm you, plans to give you hope and a future.*" Jeremiah 29:11.

I am always in awe of God bringing people and situations together at the precise moment in His plans. I needed discipleship and training and attended a course on healing at Ellel's Glyndley Manor at Pevensey, near Eastbourne.

I had booked a single room as I usually did on those weekends. So I wasn't too pleased to learn that I had been given a room with two other ladies. "Oh no" I thought, "no privacy and not one but two others!"

But God knew what He had purposed in this 'inconvenient' arrangement. Beryl and Joyce were delightful roommates, so caring and considerate, friendly and fun. Over the weekend, I felt closely bonded with them, and a relationship grew that continues to this day.

When Beryl laid her hands on me in prayer, she amazed me by saying: "Ah, a fruitful branch."

Four years after that weekend, I was experiencing emotional problems with looking after my elderly father and our relationship had become difficult. I knew I needed counselling. Beryl and Joyce had founded the 'Oasis Community Trust', a counselling ministry in Kent so I hurried down to Kent to see Beryl and to pour out my heart to her.

To know Beryl and Joyce is one of God's Divine appointments. Beryl felt she was to become my Spiritual Mentor and so began a number of years of visiting her in Kent once a month, sometimes for a day, sometimes for a weekend to keep 'short accounts' with God by dealing with areas in my life that were under the Lord's scrutiny and needed dealing with.

She was and still is a treasure, a fountain of the Lord's wisdom. He spoke powerfully through her, putting His finger on areas of sin, wrong thinking and behaviour, insecurity, confusion, rebellion – any obstacles getting in the way of my walk with Jesus.

Beryl's close walk with Jesus gave her great revelation and knowledge and I knew I was in the Lord's Presence during those invaluable sessions.

Joyce was always faithfully there, providing a peaceful, calm environment to rest and sleep, cooking delicious meals, making endless cups of tea, giving a smile, a hug, timely words of encouragement and homemade flapjacks! A precious servant of the Lord graced with the Lord's gentleness and compassion.

They are a great partnership – each doing their part in the counselling ministry, each with a beautiful servant heart serving their Lord, helping His wounded ones to receive His healing, deliverance and wholeness.

It was God's provision of this beautiful couple, that helped me through this challenging time of growth and discipleship in my walk with the Lord.

They were releasing times, but not always easy times when addressing issues the Lord highlighted that needed to be dealt with. They were always times of wonder and amazement at the Loving-kindness, Goodness and Grace of God who cares so much for us that He won't leave us where we are, but moves us on, to transform us and make us more like Himself.

Thank you, Beryl and Joyce, through the Lord you have had a very deep impact on my life.

Chapter 3

Early days

For You created my inmost being;
You knit me together in my mother's womb...
My frame was not hidden from you
When I was
made in the secret place.
When I was woven together in the depths of the earth,
Your eyes saw my unformed body.
All the days ordained for me
were written in Your book
before one of them came to be.
Psalm 139:13,15,16.

Before I formed you in the womb I knew you,
before you were born I set you apart.
Jeremiah 1:5

Our God is so vast and unfathomable to our understanding – He **knows** each one of us and even more remarkable, He knew us before we were formed in the womb, He knew us before time began, He knows the plans He has for us, and, as He said to Jeremiah, He appoints us to do good works before we have come into existence.

So, it is no surprise that before Tony and I even knew God, He brought about the circumstances that would lead to the work He was calling us to do.

We had married in 1970. Tony worked for B.O.A.C. and I had left teaching to work for International Reservations (a computerised hotel booking agency). Both of us were working in Victoria, London. We had rented a small, unfurnished apartment in Hammersmith and drove together to work.

I remember clearly the evening in 1972 when Tony came to pick me up from the office and said, "How do you fancy going to Israel for three months!" Wow, how wonderful. That sounded great. What an opportunity! I was delighted.

At the time Tony was training staff to use the new Departure Control computer system. El Al (Israel's airline) had bought the system and now needed training for their staff in Israel.

We were treated like V.I.P.s when we arrived at Lod Airport, as it was at the time. General Manager, Raffi, met us from the aircraft with a buggy and got us through arrivals and to our hotel in record time. He and his colleague, Avi, became close friends and we integrated into Israeli society.

Little did we realise that thirty years later we would be called to begin the work of the Mount Moriah Trust in Israel to help His people. That was our first visit to Israel. As we drove around the country each Shabbat with Avi as our guide, we were astounded to see all the places from the Bible – Jerusalem, Bethlehem, Beersheba, Hebron, Nazareth, Cana, Capernaum, Caesarea, the Sea of Galilee, Tiberias, Ashdod, Jaffa, Ashkelon and more. We did not know our Bible well then, but these names spoke to us. The Bible took on a greater meaning. These places existed and we felt drawn to read the Bible and find out more. This first trip only lasted a month because during that time there was a strike at the airport which was not being resolved and we returned home.

In 1973, Tony was invited to return and continue with the staff training. This time the Yom Kippur War started and our trip was cancelled again. In December of that year we finally made it back to

Tel Aviv. This time we stayed for three months. Avi had searched to find us a lovely villa in Herzliya and we had a car. I would take Tony to the airport each morning, then travel to various sights around the country. Shopping was always fun and games. I do not think I ever came to terms with buying the right things for dinner! Most things were in Hebrew and I was not an experienced cook, so we ate out a lot of the time.

Tony organised a party for the El Al staff he was training at our villa on Christmas Day. We were young, accustomed to the parties we had in England with lots of alcohol and not so much to eat. We did not think to find out about Israeli culture. If we had, we would have discovered that they had no alcohol but lots of food. I should have sensed something when Klara, Raffi's wife, said "You've given yourself a lot of work, can I help you?" "Oh no", I said, "I can manage."

I went off to the local butcher for cold meats and amused him by asking for **half a gram of salami**. "Madam", he said, "you wouldn't even see that on my fingernail!" He looked at me as if I was a crazy woman, but we laughed and finally got things right. I bought salads, fruit, meat and a few cakes. Tony bought thirty bottles of wine and we felt we were ready for the party. Avi brought his record player and records for dancing. People began to arrive. In no time at all, the food disappeared, no-one drank the wine, only soft drinks and by the time everyone had arrived, there was nothing left. It looked like Biblical locusts had struck! Some people got nothing to eat – there was not a crumb, a nut, or a banana left. Amazingly, the party went with a swing. Everyone said they enjoyed themselves, but they must have gone home starving. How young and foolish we were!

We were to go back to Israel each year for another four years for Tony to continue the training. Twice Raffi got us permission to attend the Christmas Eve service in Bethlehem. He said that Tony was Head of an airline and we were Catholic and so we were allowed to go. Even then, in the seventies, grenades would go off around Manger Square and security was tight. But we met many Arabs at that time and discovered their wonderful hospitality and kindness.

God is in and over every part of our lives. The bigger events and in the smallest details. We often do not see God's Hand upon our lives until we look back in retrospect, sometimes a long time later, even many years later.

In a craft lesson at Teacher Training College where we were learning to make a collage using odd scraps of materials, the bird I chose was a 'hoopoe'. I had never heard of this bird before nor where it could be found, but looking through the illustrations I was attracted by the look of this bird. It was not until nine years later when Tony and I first went to Israel that I saw and recognised this bird in the grounds of the hotel. When someone said to me "What is that bird?" I sounded very pompous by saying "Oh, it's a hoopoe."

The collage of the hoopoe survived for thirty-seven years. My Mum had it in the grate of the fire in the 'front room', the best room in the house, used only on special occasions or when guests came. It was only thrown out when the house was cleared and sold.

I had not realised all those years before that I had chosen to create in collage the national bird of Israel. I see God in that choice, a small but significant pointer on the path He was leading me.

We often do not see His outworking in our lives, especially when we are not walking with Him, as I was not at that time, but He is there in the weaving together of every detail and event in our lives.

His omniscience is truly awe-inspiring and takes my breath away!

Chapter 4

The Birth

Comfort, comfort My People Isaiah 40:1

In August 2001 the Lord told me He was "birthing" the work – nine months later it was born just as He said it would be.

We had been told that it could take up to fifteen months for everything to go through the Charity Commission, but the Lord was over His Work and the application went through in eight weeks! We received confirmation that 'The Mount Moriah Trust' had become a registered charity on 28th May 2002. We didn't receive the letter until after this date, but at the end of May, I believed in faith that the Trust had been birthed and I knelt in praise and thanksgiving to the Lord for fulfilling His Word. Then the letter arrived confirming our May registration.

He is so trustworthy and true to His promise that I knew in my spirit that His Word had accomplished what He purposed.

My Word that goes out from My Mouth:
It will not return to Me empty,
but will accomplish what I desire
and achieve the purpose for which I sent it.
Isaiah 55:11

He gave us Scriptures for the foundation of the Work:

Comfort, comfort My People, says your God. Isaiah 40:1.

For if the Gentiles have shared in the Jews' spiritual blessings, they **owe it** *to the Jews to share with them their material blessings.* Romans 15:27 [Emphasis added].

Jesus said – *I AM the Provider, I AM Jehovah Jireh.*

Earlier in 1999, the Lord had whispered into my spirit – *"Comfort, comfort My People."* At the time I was working with Ellel Ministries as a trainee counsellor. I assumed that God was speaking about working as a counsellor to help those in need and felt I was on the right track to achieve His purposes for me. I did not press into God and ask Him exactly what He meant! It seemed obvious to me! Such pride! Then, in September 1999, circumstances in our lives changed and my elderly father came to live with us. He was suffering from Parkinson's Disease and needed increasing care, which meant I was less able to be involved with healing retreats and ministry appointments at Ellel as I had been.

I felt totally confused. I was so sure that God was calling me to work with Ellel Ministries. We were to learn

1. to enquire more deeply about His plans, not to assume that we know what He is doing or where we are heading;
2. to wait for the Lord's timing;
3. to realise there will be tests and trials along the way;
4. to trust Him no matter what happens. That He alone knows the way we should take.

Easy? No, these lessons are difficult and learned slowly, with many painful disappointments and misunderstandings along the way. God allows us to make mistakes and take wrong turnings as it is all part of the training. God is Sovereign, He is in control. He knows the way we should take and even if we make an unnecessary detour, He will gently bring us back on track, if we are prepared to listen and walk humbly with Him.

My father died in October 2001 at the age of 93, a couple of months after we had received the vision of the work.

God's timing is so amazing. We were beginning the Mount Moriah Trust. I did not return to work with Ellel Ministries but was now free to follow this new call of God on our lives. Those two years had been difficult ones, changing our lives and bringing all our plans to a standstill, but God used this valley as a door of hope to the future: *I will make the Valley of Achor (trouble) a door of hope.* Hosea 2:15.

We know that God's work done in His way, in His timing will never lack His support. We were learning that this work is not ours but His. He had said:

"I AM The Mount Moriah Trust – it is all about Me,
My Heart for My People. Follow where I lead."

It was remarkably comforting to know that He was in total control of this work and we were invited to co-work with Him as He directed.

He told us that we were not to ask for money. We were to bring our needs to Him, and the Holy Spirit would touch hearts to give. It was all the Lord's work. The vision was His and the outworking would be His.

As David Davis said in his book *The Road to Carmel*: "I knew I had to release it all, to let go of the vision and let God have His way."

We too, had to do this. In fact, it is a continual process – letting go and letting God take control. Our part is to love God, obey and serve Him. We were reminded of the words given to Joshua as the Israelites were beginning their lives in the Promised Land –

Be very careful ... to love the Lord your God, to walk in all His ways, to obey His commands, to hold fast to Him and to serve Him with all your heart and all your soul. Joshua 22:5

Choose for yourselves this day whom you will serve ... But as for me and my household, we will serve the Lord. Joshua 24:15

We had chosen to love and obey the Lord, to serve Him with all our heart and all our soul, to walk in all His ways.

Chapter 5

The Biblical Significance of Mount Moriah

Then God said, "Take your son, your only son, whom you love-Isaac-and go to the region of Moriah." Genesis 22:2

Then Solomon began to build the temple of the LORD in Jerusalem on Mount Moriah, where the LORD had appeared to his father David. Chronicles 3:1

The name Mount Moriah Trust was not a name that we chose, it was given to us by God when He told us to start the work: *"you are to call it the Mount Moriah Trust".* The name has great significance for the charity as "Moriah" in Hebrew means "God Provides". The name demonstrates that this is His work and that He is the provider.

Mount Moriah is a very significant place. It was the place that Abraham was told to take his son Isaac to be sacrificed and the place where the ram was provided as the substitute sacrifice instead of Isaac. It was the place where Solomon built the Temple for the Lord and is the place where the Muslims built the Dome of the Rock Mosque, taking great pains to ensure that it was built exactly where the Temple had stood.

Some people may ask "what's in a name?" but in Hebrew names and their meanings are so important. The name Mount Moriah is so significant that it warrants sharing the following Bible study with you.

On 20th May 2007 Pastor John Angliss invited us to give a

presentation of the work to the South of Reading Christian Fellowship. It was a special service to commission us to take the ministry to a wider audience.

Pastor John had prepared his message for the morning, but during worship, the Holy Spirit spoke to him telling him to speak instead about the meaning and significance of Mount Moriah in the Word of God. Obediently he hurried off to find his notes and laid aside the message he had planned for that day. With thanks to the Holy Spirit and to Pastor John, we look into the Biblical meaning of Mount Moriah, the name the Lord gave to the Trust and we can see its significance.

MOUNT MORIAH

The meaning and significance of the name.
"Moriah" in Hebrew means *"God/Yah Provides"*

Genesis 22

Abraham is brought to the supreme test of his life when God calls him to take his promised son Isaac to Mount Moriah to sacrifice him as a burnt offering. This is a type, shadow and representation of Christ's Crucifixion more than 2,000 years before it happens.

— Abraham, the **father** taking his **son** to sacrifice Genesis 22:2	— God, the **Father** taking His **Son** to the Cross Matthew 3:17
— Isaac was **supernaturally** born to Sarah in her old age	— Jesus was **supernaturally** conceived by the Holy Spirit
— **Unity** between the father and son: *the two of them went on together* v.6,8	— **Unity** between God and His Son: *I and the Father are One* John 10:30
— the **third day** *Abraham looked up* v.4	— On the **third day** He rose from the dead
— **Wood** for the offering – *the wood for the burnt offering... placed on his son Isaac* v.6	— The **Cross** placed on Jesus

- **Burden** of Isaac bearing the wood
- **Resurrection:** Abraham believed God would resurrect his son
- **Obedience** of Isaac to be the sacrifice

- **Fire:** *he himself carried the fire.* v.6 Fire = the Holy Spirit

- **Burden** of Jesus bearing the Cross
- Jesus is the **Resurrection:** *I am the Resurrection.* John 11:25
- **Obedience** of Jesus to be the living sacrifice *He humbled Himself and became obedient to death – even death on a Cross* Philippians 2:8
- **Fire:** *God is a consuming fire* Deuteronomy 4:4; Hebrews 12:29

By faith Abraham, when God tested him, offered Isaac as a sacrifice. He who had embraced the promises was about to sacrifice his one and only son, even though God had said to him, "It is through Isaac that your offspring will be reckoned." Abraham reasoned that God could even raise the dead, and so in a manner of speaking he did receive Isaac back from death. Hebrews 11:17–19

Jesus said: "Your father Abraham rejoiced as he looked forward to my coming. He saw it and was glad." John 8:56 (NLT).

Abraham saw it by the eye of faith; by faith he had the revelation of Jesus, therefore he could entrust his son to God.

- God's **provision** of a ram v.13
- God's **provision** of the Lamb of God *"the Lamb that was slain from the creation of the world"* Revelation 13:8

Mount Moriah as we have seen is:

- a place of **sacrifice** and **offering**
  Christ loved us and gave Himself up for us as a fragrant offering and sacrifice to God. Ephesians 5:2

- a place of **substitution**
  Jesus died for us as a substitute for us, for our sins.

  God made Him who had no sin to be sin for us. 2 Corinthians 5:21

He Himself bore our sins in His body on the tree. 1 Peter 2:24

the Lord Jesus Christ, who gave Himself for our sins. Galatians 1:4

Christ was sacrificed once to take away the sins of many people. Hebrews 9:28

He is the atoning sacrifice for our sins. 1 John 2:2

- a place of **provision**
  God provided His own Son, the Lamb of God. Jesus made provision for our sins.

- a place of **atonement**
  King David sinned by taking a census of the fighting men without collecting the atonement money which each man should have offered.

Then the Lord said to Moses, "When you take a census of the Israelites to count them, each one must pay the Lord a ransom for his life at the time he is counted. Then no plague will come on them when you number them." Exodus 30:12

The atonement cannot be omitted, it is not possible to by-pass the blood and be right with God.
God offered David the choice of three punishments:
- three years of famine;
- three months of being swept away before their enemies with their swords
- three days of plague in the land

David put himself into the hands of the Lord who sent a pestilence on Israel and 70,000 men die. Gad told David to build an altar to the Lord on the threshing floor of Araunah, the Jebusite. 1 Chronicles 21:18. He bought the threshing floor and sacrificed burnt offerings and fellowship offerings. The Angel of the Lord put his sword back into its sheath, 1 Chronicles 21:27 and the plague ended.

We see again that Mount Moriah is a place of **sacrifice** and **offering, sin**, **judgement** and **mercy**.

It is a place of **purchase**.

The threshing floor was the site of the Temple. David paid Araunah 600 shekels of gold for the site. He insisted on paying the full price 1 Chronicles 21:24-25 just as Jesus paid the full price when He bought us with His precious blood.

On Mount Moriah the Temple of the Living God was built by King Solomon.

> *Then Solomon began to build the Temple of the Lord in Jerusalem on Mount Moriah, where the Lord had appeared to his father David. It was on the threshing floor of Araunah the Jebusite, the place provided by David.* 2 Chronicles 3:1

Mount Moriah is a place of **purchase** so that we can be a temple of the Living God.

> *In Him the whole building is joined together and rises to become a holy temple in the Lord. And in Him you too are being built together to become a dwelling in which God lives by His Spirit.* Ephesians 2:21-22

Mount Moriah is a place of **progress** and **growth**.

> *He began to build the Temple of the Lord.* 1 Kings 6:1

> *So Solomon built the Temple and completed it.* v.14

> *Jesus is the author and finisher of our faith.* Hebrews 12:2

He who began a good work in you will carry it on to completion until the day of Christ Jesus. Philippians 1:6

The building is a picture of the growth of the believer and of the church. Every believer is another stone in the Holy building. We are growing and progressing. We are the living stones.

As you come to Him, the living Stone... you also, like living stones, are being built into a spiritual house to be a holy priesthood, offering spiritual sacrifices acceptable to God through Jesus Christ. 1 Peter 1:4-5

In conclusion, Mount Moriah speaks of Jesus and His work:
- The Father offering up His Son
- The sacrifice of Jesus on the Cross
- Substitution: Jesus was the scapegoat
- Salvation: that Jesus bought for us on Calvary
- Atonement: the price has been fully paid by Jesus
- Sin/Judgement/Mercy: Jesus became sin for us and reconciled us to God
- Purchase: we have been bought by the precious blood of Jesus
- The Temple : Jesus is the Living Stone, the Cornerstone
- Progress/growth: begun and completed by Jesus

Thank you, Pastor John
Thank you, HOLY SPIRIT.

Chapter 6

God's Teaching About Israel

His people, His treasured possession. Deuteronomy 7:6.

Each step of the way on this journey has been a work of God, to achieve His purposes. As a new believer in 1993 I knew nothing about Israel and the significance of the land and the Jewish people. But the Lord set about teaching me His Heart of love for His ancient Covenant people and through His Word, He showed me that He has plans and purposes for His Jewish people that will bring blessing to the world.

At the Kerith Centre Church the Lord gave me a Prayer Partner who was passionate about Israel. At first I did not understand what the Jews had to do with me, what Israel meant for me as a Christian. I had become a believer and follower of Jesus and that was enough for me. But God had other ideas. Through this woman, the Lord began to open my eyes to His Word on His everlasting love for the Jewish people, His everlasting Covenant with them, their importance and significance in the End Time plans of God.

I discovered that the Kerith Centre Church believed in Replacement Theology; a belief that God has finished with Israel and the Jews. How incredible that it was through the Holy Spirit and His leading that I learned about Israel and the Jewish people within this church that denied that the nation had any special significance to God and His plans!

How absolutely incredible God is!

Nothing and no-one is an obstacle to His Word, His Plans, His Purposes. His Power, Authority and Sovereignty are supreme in any and every circumstance.

I AM the Lord, the God of all mankind. Is anything too hard for Me? Jeremiah 32:27.

Is anything too hard for the Lord? Genesis 18:14.

The Lord showed me that through the Jews, He revealed who He is to mankind, His ways and His commandments. All the prophets and apostles were Jewish and the church started with the Jews before Apostle Paul took the word to the Gentiles.

For if the Gentiles have shared in the Jews' spiritual blessings, they owe it to the Jews to share with them their material blessings. Romans 15:27.

The Spiritual blessings that we have received from the Jews:
- We have received the Messiah, our Saviour and Lord;
- Through Israel God has revealed who He is;
- We see the relationship He requires with us;
- We know His commands, His ways, His covenants;
- We learn His names through which we see His character;
- We have received the Word of God – the Bible;
- The heritage and roots of the Christian faith are Jewish.

Today these facts are being largely ignored in the majority of churches. Some have followed in the steps of the early church fathers who believed the Jews were Christ-killers and God had finished with them. Some have taken sides with the Palestinians, believing that they are oppressed by Israel and have lost their land to the Jewish nation. Some are without understanding, indifferent or lukewarm about the situation in the Middle East. Some are angry with Israel who appear to be the aggressors, even thinking that Israel is an apartheid state!

Very few study the Bible to search for God's Word on the subject or try to find out the truth about the situation in Israel. Some are confused because they feel the Word can be interpreted in different ways to mean different things. Some are happy to leave the subject alone and avoid controversy, concentrating instead on other Christian issues in their walk with God.

Why would God choose a nation for His purposes, one whom He loved, write their history in the Old Testament, which makes up three-quarters of the Bible, send His Son as the Jewish Messiah who forgave them from the Cross, only to finish with them! Is that the heart of God?

The Israelites angered and grieved Him, but He knew from the beginning they would do this. But His unfathomable, amazing Grace, which saves us all as sinners, will also save His people, the Jews. *"His gifts and His call are irrevocable."* (Romans 11:29). Like Apostle Paul, my heart's cry is that we look at what God is saying in the whole counsel of God about His land, His people, His plans for them and His purposes for them in the End Times, the Tribulation and the Millennial Kingdom.

It is all there in His Word! The Truth. Our part is to seek the Lord for revelation and He will give understanding and show us His Heart.

We must be wary that we are not on a collision course with Almighty God. We can so easily buy into the lie of Satan who hates the Jewish people and the land of Israel. He knows that the Lord Jesus Christ will return to the Mount of Olives at the end of the Tribulation to set up His Kingdom for one thousand years and that will be the end of Satan's rule.

If there is no Jerusalem, no Israel, no Jewish people, God's Word will not be fulfilled. Satan will have a reprieve from his death sentence given to him in Genesis 3:15:

He (Jesus) *will crush your head* (Satan's authority). [Author's comments added]

But God's Word stands for ever; the Lord is coming to reign for one thousand years on earth, and during that time Satan will be bound.

> *On that day His feet will stand on the Mount of Olives, east of Jerusalem...* Zechariah 14:4.

> *And I saw an angel coming down out of Heaven, having the key to the Abyss and holding in his hand a great chain. He seized the dragon, that ancient serpent, who is the devil, or Satan, and bound him for a thousand years.* Revelation 20:1-2.

Satan's final doom –

> *When the thousand years are over, Satan will be released from his prison and will go out to deceive the nations ...... to gather them for battle .... They marched across the breadth of the earth and surrounded the camp of God's people, the city He loves. But fire came down from heaven and devoured them. And the devil, who deceived them, was thrown into the lake of burning sulphur .... To be tormented day and night for ever and ever.* Revelation 20:7-10

We need to be wary of Satan's deception. As believers we will not be thrown into the Lake of Fire, but he can distort our thinking to come into line with his about Israel and the Jewish people which stands opposed to the Word of God and His truth.

Chapter 7

The God of the Unexpected

He will guide you into all truth John 16:13

God's commands can seem strange and unusual. One day in my quiet time the Lord said *"I want you to take a balloon flight."*

That was a strange instruction. I certainly had not been thinking about such a thing, so I knew it wasn't my thinking. Why would the Lord want us to go up in a balloon?

A couple of days later, how amazed we were to receive in the post a discounted offer from Virgin to – guess what – book a balloon flight! I knew then it was from the Lord and we booked our flight.

A couple of times the flight had to be re-scheduled because of adverse weather conditions, but finally on a beautiful September afternoon in 2006, at Henley, we took off with fourteen other passengers. It was an incredible experience. As we went higher, it was so peaceful and quiet, only the occasional sound of the flame heating the air in the balloon. We understood from the pilot that he really had no control over the direction in which we travel. The wind determined which way we went. At one point we were travelling too close to Heathrow Airport and we had to come down in a field before we made national news for bringing Heathrow to a halt! But the farmer was not amused; he had not given permission to land and said we had to take off, out of his land! We finally came down on a piece of very stony, rocky ground, and this time the land owner, having been placated by the offer of free tickets, said it was okay for us all to disembark and pack up the balloon.

The Lord had shown us that the wind that controlled our direction and where we went, was like the Holy Spirit. He would direct us and take us where He wanted us to go. He would control the direction of the work. He would protect us from the dangers of going the wrong way. The Lord showed us that as with the balloon flight, the higher we went, the peace and tranquillity increased; so it is in our walk with Him. The higher we go, the greater the stillness and peace.

He showed us that as we went higher, our perspective on everything changed. We soared over the countryside, the earth and everything in it seemed smaller and less significant. This is how it is when we soar higher with the Lord, above our circumstances. A great place to be! By flying too close to Heathrow airspace, He showed us that if we stray into the wrong territory, there will be repercussions, and dangers. We need to keep out of the enemy's territory by staying close to the Lord and to walk in all His ways, otherwise we will run into difficulty and opposition and certain trouble.

Coming down in an unauthorised area caused hostility and aggression; we were not welcome. The Lord showed us that we must beware of straying into areas where He has not directed us to go. It will cause unnecessary detours and vexation and certain opposition.

The final landing in the rocky field showed us that we need the Lord's guidance on every step of our journey with Him. He will steer us through the rocky places, the difficult times that will come. But He will lead us through the tough times as we lean on Him.

The Hebrew words for the Holy Spirit are: *"Ruach Ha Kodesh"* which translates as *"the Holy Wind of God."* This conveys the meaning of the experience so well and describes how He would lead the Mount Moriah Trust.

The flame of the balloon spoke of the power of the Holy Spirit. We had been told to wear a hat or head covering to protect against being burnt by the flame if we stood near it. The trip was a very graphic picture of how the Trust would operate using the wind and the fire of the Holy Spirit.

The flight was a delight. We were given a certificate to remember it by and the Lord's vibrant teaching lesson was memorable, a never-to-be forgotten practical object lesson of His Divine oversight.

Interestingly, we have never received another balloon offer since. God used that offer to bring about His purposes!

Renewal of our Marriage Vows

I make all things new. Revelation 21:5 (NKJV)

Before the Lord gave the call to begin the Mount Moriah Trust, He said that we were to renew our marriage vows. After thirty years of wear and tear, He wanted to make our marriage new before we embarked on His work together. Just as we are made new when we are born again, our marriage was to be made new for this new phase that was coming in our lives. We did not know about the work at that point but we obeyed what he was asking of us.

We were approaching our thirtieth (Pearl) wedding anniversary in 2000 and had decided to celebrate it on the Isle of Wight. Dad had to go into a care home again, but in fact, he enjoyed being looked after by all the young carers and it was not a problem.

We stayed at the Rylstone Manor Hotel in Shanklin. It was a lovely Victorian house set in beautiful Rylstone Gardens. We had no idea where we would go to church, whether we could find a Minister to renew our vows or if it could be arranged at such short notice.

But the Lord had already arranged it. He had all the details worked out and in His amazing way, made it all possible, simply and beautifully. As we drove around Shanklin looking for churches, we passed the Methodist Church and felt that this was the one. It was later that we remembered we were married in a Methodist church in 1970. We attended the service on Sunday and the message was about Covenant and Renewal! God was certainly speaking to us. After the service we met their retired Minister, the Rev. Douglas Brown who said he was very happy to renew our marriage vows on our anniversary; 29th August at 2.00 p.m.

At this service Rev. Douglas prayed and read passages from the Bible and we renewed our vows to each other. He spoke of our commitment as friend and supporter to one another. We asked for God's help. We received His blessing on us and on our marriage. It was absolutely lovely. As we said goodbye to Rev. Douglas, I said, "God has led us here." He said, "I think He has."

God's choice of Minister was perfect. He was such a special person, gentle, kind, radiating Christ's love. He had ended the service with the Aaronic Blessing (Numbers 6:22–27), which, on reflection, was so significant in light of the coming call to work within Israel. The service was very moving and we were all powerfully aware of the Lord's Presence. In a letter we received later Rev. Douglas wrote:

> "It was a joy and a privilege to conduct a simple private service for the Renewal of your Marriage Vows on the actual anniversary of your marriage. I felt the Lord's Presence when we were together in church and am delighted you did also."

That same night there was hymn singing at the Rylstone Park Bandstand. There were so few people who came. Two men from the Full Gospel Business Men's Fellowship International were speaking. As I went forward for prayer afterwards one of them said "The Lord has a high place for you. You have been given a high calling, but don't be afraid, Jesus is with you."

I was astounded by these words and received them from the Lord in humble gratitude and amazement, though I did not understand what they meant. What a day it had been!

God had been teaching us about Covenants during these few days away:

1. I remembered that it was on the Isle of Wight that I had first

made a covenant with Jesus forty years ago (though I had broken that covenant);

2. The Marriage Covenant made with Tony was thirty years ago. God was renewing and strengthening the Covenant and commitment we had made to each other before He gave us the work.

God was revealing His Redemption, Restoration and Renewal. What a gracious God!

Chapter 8

Obedience

Observe the commands of the LORD your God, walking in obedience to him and revering him. Deuteronomy 8:6

God requires our obedience to His call, His commands, His will. He doesn't ask us to do anything that He hasn't done Himself. The greatest act of obedience is seen in our Lord Jesus Christ. He willingly obeyed His Father's will to come to earth to die on the cross, to take our sins, our sinful nature upon Himself and defeat the power of evil.

The Son of God willingly left His glory in Heaven; what amazing obedience!

Jesus loved the Father and obeyed Him. Love and obedience go together. Like the song from the fifties, 'Love and marriage go together like a horse and carriage, you can't have one without the other.' Love and obedience are like that; you cannot have one without the other.

Jesus says **twice** in John 14:

If you love Me, you will obey what I command. John 14:15
If anyone loves Me, he will obey My teaching. John 14:23

And again in John 15:

If you obey My commands, you will remain in My love, just as

I have obeyed My Father's commands and remain in His love.
John 15:10.

God values obedience very highly. It is at the top of His list of values.

God is all-wise and all-knowing. His ways and thoughts are perfect. They are higher than our ways and thoughts (Isaiah 55:8-9). Therefore, we can trust God as He calls us to obey Him. He is not a dictator, but a loving Father. He wants the best for us. He knows what is best.

We can miss the perfect timing of God by disobedience. He knows what will happen if we do not obey Him – there are always consequences when we disobey.

Before the work began, the Lord tested me to see if I would obey His commands. I heard the Lord say to me: *"Go to another hairdresser."* Like Saul, I disobeyed. I began to think about it and decided it probably was not the voice of the Lord. I reasoned my way out of it. Why would God worry about which hairdresser I went to? So I went as usual to have my hair permed. I had been having my hair permed for more than twenty years, but on this occasion, as the perm lotion was applied, my skin began to burn; all around my hairline and neck was very red and uncomfortable.

The awful thing was, I did not want to relate what had happened with God and my disobedience, so I went back a few months later for another perm. The hairdresser was very careful this time and I was covered in cotton wool around my neck and hairline. But this time God turned up the heat. The same thing happened, my skin burning, red and very uncomfortable. My clothes were soaked when the perm lotion was rinsed off, making me feel really uncomfortable, and worse still, I began to feel very sick. None of these things had ever happened before in all those years. I had to tell the hairdresser to hurry up the process because I felt very unwell. When I came home I had to lie down and it took the rest of the day to recover. I finally got the message; I had disobeyed God! He had good reasons for what He asked me to do. I had to learn to do what He said even though I didn't understand why.

Trust in the Lord with all your heart and lean not on your own understanding. Proverbs 3:5.

I later heard that the salon was incorporating treatments from Far Eastern religions into their style of hairdressing. This was displeasing to the Lord and He will not tolerate the influence of other gods in His children.

I still had to learn that when God says something, just do it!

A while later I was given instructions, disobeyed again and paid the penalty. The church decided that all members should share in the task of regularly cleaning the building. I signed up to do my part and was then surprised to hear the Lord say: *"You have not enquired of Me, I haven't asked you to do this."* On this occasion, I had difficulty saying to the church, I would not be able to do the cleaning. Like Saul, *"I was afraid of the people and I gave in to them."* 1 Samuel 15:24. I was pleasing people rather than God. I cleaned the church windows.

The next day, I had such a pain in my chest, I thought I was going to have a heart attack! Tony and I were going to Israel in just a couple of days, so I thought, I have got to go to the doctor. When she examined me, she said, "What have you been doing?" When she said that, I knew it was the Lord confronting me with what I had done contrary to His word. There was not much wrong with me, only muscle pain. After that, I spoke to the Pastor and he understood and released me from that duty.

From those two examples, I saw that it is essential to obey God. With obedience, we save ourselves and others a lot of difficulty, upset, delay, disappointment, even pain and enemy attack. God blesses trust and obedience. It is all part of loving Him.

As Jesus's mother Mary said to the servants at the wedding in Cana: *"Do whatever He tells you."* John 2:5. I was learning, albeit slowly, that listening to God, obeying, acting on what He says, willingly and completely, without knowing why sometimes, in simple trust and faith in the Almighty is an act of love.

Chapter 9

Cleansing

Wash away all my iniquity and cleanse me from my sin
Psalm 51:2

*Purify me from my sins, and I will be clean; wash me, and I
will be whiter than snow.* Psalm 51:7 (NLT)

The Lord is a Holy God and He calls us to be holy – *"Be holy because
I AM holy."* 1 Peter 1:16

We cannot do this without the Holy Spirit. Little by little we are changed by His transforming love and His transforming grace. We discovered that the Lord not only wants to cleanse us, but also our homes and where we live.

In the beginning of the Ministry, the Lord put His finger on the areas of our home and garden which were displeasing to Him.

Throughout our years of travel, Tony and I had collected various artefacts and ornaments. But the Lord began to highlight certain objects and as we looked at them more closely we saw what they represented. Some were Indian gods and goddesses, some were from Far-Eastern religions. We had a large collection of frogs and owls of all kinds, glass, pottery, wood. Friends knew we liked them and would buy us gifts of every imaginable size, shape and material. We had a veritable **plague** of them in our home and garden!

We realised that they were displeasing to the Lord so we collected them up, put them in boxes and put them in the loft. In truth, I couldn't bear to throw them away. They were at least out of the way up there, or so I thought.

But God wanted rid of them and destroyed. He knew the spiritual significance of these objects and that the enemy of our souls has a hold over us through them.

God had sent a plague of frogs on the Egyptians –

Against all the gods of Egypt I will execute judgement; I AM the Lord. Exodus 12:12. (NKJV)

Heqet is an Egyptian goddess of fertility, represented in the form of a frog. To the Egyptians, the frog was an ancient symbol of fertility, related to the annual flooding of the Nile.

In Revelation, when the bowls of God's Wrath are being poured on the earth, John *"saw three evil spirits that looked like frogs ..... they are spirits of demons performing miraculous signs."* Revelation 16:13-14.

Owls are symbols in witchcraft and used in satanic rituals and rites. God wanted all these things out of our home, for our protection and to release any footholds the enemy may have had in our lives through them.

It must be said that God has nothing against frogs and owls in the natural world – they are His creation. His anger is against the enemy, Satan, who has used them as symbols of evil and idolatry.

God did not want them in the loft. After one of our trips away, we came home to discover that the door to the loft had so forcibly come down, it had gouged a piece out of the wall on the landing. We got the message! We knew God had powerfully opened the door for us to remove them. We also needed to repair and decorate the wall. We had finally learned our lesson!

Rosie, a dear friend and supporter of the work whom I had met in Jerusalem at the David Hathaway Conference, came for coffee one morning and was horrified to see in our garden a statue of the god

Pan playing a flute. She could hardly believe that Tony and I had such a thing.

> Pan is a god of the wild. He is considered to be one of the
> oldest Greek gods. He is associated with nature, wooded areas
> and pasturelands. Worship of Pan centred in nature often in
> caves or grottos. He ruled over shepherds, hunters and rustic
> music. He was often in the company of the wood nymphs and
> other deities of the forest. (greekgodsandgoddesses.net)

It is where the word 'panic' comes from. I could see we needed to get rid of it; an innocent looking statue with spiritual undertones. When Ron, our gardener, came to tidy our garden, I asked if he could take away the statue of Pan. He knew Tony and I were Christians and I explained to him that this statue represented a false god and was displeasing to the Lord and therefore could not be sold or passed on but had to be smashed and destroyed.

He understood, put the statue into the back of his Range Rover and took it away. The next time he came he explained what had happened when he got home. As he reversed into his drive he heard a loud crunch and wondered what he had hit. He got out but could not bear to look to see what damage he had done. He went indoors, made himself a cup of tea and worked in the garden before he could bring himself to look at what he had done to his car. Amazingly, he could find nothing wrong. But he knew he had to destroy the statue. The Lord had shown him very clearly it was to be broken up and taken to the rubbish tip, just in case he had any ideas of keeping it!

After these incidents and understanding the significance of certain objects that we may think are harmless, but in actual fact have spiritual roots in the occult or false religions, the Lord brought two separate people to me. One with a ring, another with a necklace that they felt unhappy with and were not sure why. They asked if I could explain the meaning or significance of what they thought was a type of Christian Cross. Both these items displayed an 'ankh'; a cross with a loop on the top which was a symbol of life in Egyptian culture.

The Ankh is a cross with a loop at the top sometimes ornamented with symbols or decorative flourishes but most often simply a plain gold cross. The symbol is an Egyptian hieroglyph for "life" or "breath of life" and, as the Egyptians believed that one's earthly journey was only part of an eternal life, the ankh symbolizes both mortal existence and the afterlife. It is one of the most ancient symbols of Egypt, often seen with the *djed* and *was* symbols, carried by a multitude of the Egyptian gods in tomb paintings and inscriptions and worn by Egyptians as an amulet. (ancient.eu/ankh)

These crosses are mistakenly used as symbols of the cross of Christ. **But nothing could be further from the truth.** Satan is the arch deceiver and lures many into deception. Jesus said of him:

> *... there is no truth in him. When he lies he speaks his native language, for he is a liar and the father of lies.* John 8:44

Each person was happy to get rid of the piece of jewellery and realised the Lord was pinpointing the spiritual meaning and influence behind the items.

On one of our trips to Israel we visited the son of a precious brother in the Lord who had an IT business that was helping us with our website. He is a Christian but a close friend of his had given him a Buddha statue. As I had been shown the error of having the statue of Pan in the garden, now the Lord was allowing me to point out the offending statue in our friend's garden. At first he did not understand why he should get rid of it. He liked it as an ornament and a good friend of his whom he trusted had given it as a gift. I gave him the Scripture:

Throw away the foreign gods that are among you. Joshua 24:23.

Later we explained to his father what we had seen in the garden, knowing that he would know what had to be done and his son began to see that foreign gods are detestable to Almighty God and he finally got rid of it. He was rewarded with an upturn in his business!

There seems to be 'plague' of Buddhas in our country. They are prominent features in garden centres and in gardens in the UK.

When we visit families in the Arab towns of Israel, we see many statues of Mary and baby Jesus and shrines to Mary. They can be inside or outside the home. Many Arabs come to faith through the Catholic Church which has deified Mary, the mother of Christ. They have failed to see that there is a Holy Trinity; Father, Son and Holy Spirit. God will not give His Glory to another, and Mary, though a highly favoured woman who gave birth to the Lord Jesus, remains an earthly vessel, who should not be prayed to or worshipped. God says:

I will not give my Glory to another. Isaiah 48:11. (NKJV)

Tony and I are concerned as we visit these towns, that these figurines of Mary bring with them a spirit of idolatry that has profound influence on the lives of those who are inadvertently worshipping another god. It seems innocent to worship the mother of Jesus, but God says:

You shall have no other gods before Me... You shall not bow down to them or worship them; for I, the Lord your God, am a jealous God. Exodus 20:3,5.

Do the idols of Mary, which are prayed to and worshipped, bring with them consequences in the lives of believers in the Lord Jesus

Christ? We rather believe so and long for the day when these figures and shrines will disappear. Nevertheless, there is such love for Jesus among the believers. But no-one else has the Power and Authority to give life, to heal, to comfort, to cleanse, to save.

Praise God that He wants us to enjoy complete freedom from any deceptive spiritual forces that the enemy delights to use.

Praise Him that He deals with these areas gradually. He does not expect our lives to be perfectly cleansed before He will use us. We come to Christ just as we are and He undertakes to clean us up and set us free from all that encaptured us whilst we were living in the Kingdom of darkness. He wants a pure and spotless bride, but He is the Sanctifier.

We are a work in progress in the Loving Hands of the Purifier and Refiner.

Chapter 10

Divine Disciplines

He who dwells in the secret place of the Most High (El Elyon)
shall abide under the shadow of the Almighty (El Shaddai).
Psalm 91:1 (NKJV) Hebrew names added.

The Secret Place

Being in the 'secret place' with Jesus is all part of the work of the Mount Moriah Trust. To dwell in the shelter of Almighty God is not only an honour and a privilege, it is a place of intimacy with God Himself, of revelation, of knowledge and it is **the** place of safety and protection and the enemy cannot touch you there.

Is it any wonder it is high up on the list of the Lord's training disciplines?

In the eight years of training from being born again in 1993 to the call of God in 2001, spending time alone with Jesus every day had been and still is of paramount importance.

I quote from *Streams in the Desert*:

"We would be better Christians if we spent more time alone, and we would actually accomplish more if we attempted less and spent more time in isolation and quiet waiting upon God."

"Our time is never more profitably spent than when we set

aside time for quiet meditation, talking with God and looking up to Heaven."

"It may mean that we do less outward, visible work, but the work we do will have more depth and power."

Tommy Tenney in his book *The God Chasers* says:

"I encourage you to linger and soak in the Presence of the Lord at every opportunity. When you draw near to Him, don't hurry and don't rush. Realise that this is (or should be) at the top of your priority list. Let God do a deep work in your heart and life."

"The only way to the place David called 'the secret place' is through the door of focussed worship, when you lay aside every distraction and focus your body, soul and spirit upon God."

Spending time alone with God each day, sitting in His Presence to draw from His strength and life prepares us for the day ahead. The time is never wasted, though sometimes it seems an easy option to sit quietly when there are things to do. But I have always been surprised at what can be accomplished in a short time when you first take time to be with the Lord. He seems to stretch time and I never cease to be amazed at what can be achieved in a day after giving time to Him. He seems to return it in double measure!

Frederick William Farrar said of his mother who spent time with the Lord each morning: "She had drunk from 'the river of the water of life' (Revelation 22:1) and had eaten of 'the living bread that came down from heaven.'" (John 6:51) (L.B.Cowman *Streams in the Desert*)

Spending time with Jesus increases our efficiency, He has said to me: *"Because I AM Almighty God, I AM able to stretch time and arrange events in your favour. You will find that you can do **more** in **less** time, after you have spent time with Me."*

What a wonderful promise and I have found this to be true on every occasion.

It can be a great temptation to get started on your long list of things 'to do'. But if I spend time with Jesus **first**, I find that I get all the things on the list completed in a much shorter time; even **more** in **less** time! Amazing!

Jesus has given us the Holy Spirit to live within us, therefore it is not difficult to commune with the Person, the Divine Being who has taken up residence within us. He does not come and go, visiting occasionally. He lives in our spirit at all times! Incredible? It certainly is, but if we understand this, it is not difficult to talk and communicate with Jesus through the Holy Spirit in us. He has made this possible because that is what He desires – to communicate with His children. What a loving Father He is. Don't be afraid or hesitant. He may speak to you through your circumstances, what you are going through at the time, or through His Word as you daily read His Scripture. You will know when He highlights a word or a passage. He also speaks directly into your spirit in an inaudible voice, but one that you can clearly hear. Write down what He says. It will certainly edify you. The Holy Spirit will always give Glory to the Lord Jesus Christ, that is His function.

In 1 Kings 19:12 God spoke to Elijah in a *"gentle whisper"* (NIV) or *"a still small voice"* (NKJV). Jeff Lucas in his book *Elijah: Anointed and Stressed describes it in this way:*

> "Some have translated this as 'the sound of gentle silence', the silent sound ... It seems to me in my experience that the voice of God is just like that: gentle, calm, solidly there, yet – was that really him?".

The Lord delights in the time you spend with Him and you will also delight in that time. You will be cleansed, healed, strengthened in His Presence. You cannot be in the presence of the Almighty God without being changed in some way. He is so mighty and powerful, you will receive His love, His joy, His peace that passes all understanding, His rest.

You will receive His guidance, His leading in any given situation. You will hear words of encouragement, rebuke, correction. He will want to bring you back to His chosen direction for you if you have strayed off course. You will feel His protection, His authority and power in every situation and you will be lifted up on wings like eagles to soar with Him.

Your time spent with Him is a privilege and an honour and will result in overflowing love of and for Him, thanksgiving, praise and worship of our Almighty and Everlasting God, Creator of heaven and earth, who dwells on high and within you and loves you with a passion, beyond our understanding.

He is coming for you, His precious bride, to live with Him for eternity!

Ask the Lord to open your ears and your heart to hear His voice. He promises:

Ask and it will be given to you... for everyone who asks receives. Matthew 7:7-8.

You do not have, because you do not ask God. James 4:2.

The quiet times we have with the Lord are times of deepening our relationship with Him and growing and maturing in our daily walk with Him. We learn invaluable lessons of perseverance and endurance. God's aim is to make us like His Son.

For me, there were times of stripping away, cleansing, healing, removing wrong thought patterns and behaviour that were displeasing to Him. Pruning can be painful when we feel the Gardener's pruning shears, but always profitable and fruitful.

I AM the true vine, and My Father is the gardener. He cuts off every branch in me that bears no fruit, while every branch that

64

does bear fruit He prunes, so that it will be even more fruitful.
John 15:1-2.

David Hathaway reminds us in one of his *Prophetic Vision Magazines*:

> Even the most famous among God's Generals have to learn
> how to fulfil the Will of God in their lives, to be obedient
> to Him, to follow Him through every success and failure,
> triumph and discouragement.
>
> True faith is expressed in faithfulness acted out in real
> life, and success comes to the one who has a deep personal
> relationship with God.
>
> Although sometimes we get discouraged and disappointed
> we need to live close enough to the Lord, to know what He
> wants, and to recognise His timing!
>
> We have got to get close enough to God to understand what
> He wants us to do, to fulfil HIS PLAN! God is the Master
> Strategist.

God desires and requires us to live closely with Him, then we are able
to **discern** His voice:

> *His sheep follow Him because they know His voice... My sheep*
> **listen** *to My voice: I know them, and they follow Me.* John
> 10:4,27.

Not only talking to God, but **listening** to Him, **hearing** His voice.

There are three voices we can hear:
  our own
  Satan's
  The Lord God Himself

He trained me to hear His voice, sometimes by listening to the voice of the enemy and learning the difference. In the beginning of my Christian life, I attended Ellel Ministries' courses either at Pierrepoint in Farnham or at Glyndley Manor, near Eastbourne. Ellel teachers would say "Go and sit quietly with the Lord and hear what He is saying to you." I was learning to listen for and listen to the voice of God from the beginning of my walk. The Lord was teaching that you listen to His voice first before you can discern other voices. I have heard it said that to know the difference between a genuine and a counterfeit bank note, you study the real thing and then you can identify the counterfeit one.

Early in this training, my mum had to undergo a minor operation, but she did need to have an anaesthetic. She was in her eighties and there is always a risk. One morning as I was praying for her, I heard a voice say to me "Your mother won't survive this operation." I was shocked and horrified by this 'revelation', but then began to feel that the Lord was preparing me in advance for what was to happen. As the day wore on, instead of feeling peaceful about this, I grew more and more agitated and seemed to be falling apart. I had no peace whatsoever, only anxiety, tears, and such indescribable sadness and fear. After prayer, I began to realise this was not from the Lord. He was testing me to understand the effect of His words on any given situation and the effect of the enemy's words.

When I visited my mum in hospital after her operation, there she was as bright as a button. She had been talking to all the patients in her ward, listening to their needs and problems and saying, "Oh, my daughter will pray for you when she comes." So, when I arrived, there was a ward of women waiting for prayer!

God had brought the situation around for His Glory and many received a special touch from Him that day. What a difference in outcome from the one the enemy had planned.

My mum had become a believer in Jesus at the age of 85, soon after I had given my life to the Lord. She had said "I want what you have" and by God's grace, I led her to the Lord. Her life changed. She found a local church to attend and it was a delight to see her grow in the Lord. How good God is. From the time she was fearful that at the age of fifteen, I was becoming a 'religious fanatic' to this moment, when God turned everything around and allowed me to play a part in her salvation! God's timing is perfect. Four years later, He was to call her home. She was so fit and well and her doctor had said that she was doing remarkably well for her age. Two days later she was taken to hospital with suspected heart problems. I was able to go with her in the ambulance.

The next day as I was driving to visit her in hospital, the Lord gently asked *"Will you release your mother to me?"* This time I knew the gentle voice of the Lord. He was graciously telling me what He was going to do. Although the tears streamed down my face, I had such peace knowing it was the Lord. Once at the hospital, my time was taken up with caring for her. She was just like her vibrant old self wanting me to bring in her make-up the next day, which would have been Christmas Day.

That night she died. Separation from someone you love and is so close, is devastating. The loss and finality of death is grievous, unbearable. But I knew she would be with the Lord and my gratitude to Him for His grace, His goodness, His timing, His love was beyond measure.

Prayer

Jesus's command was:

> *But when you pray, go into your room, close the door and pray to your Father, who is unseen. Then your Father, who sees what is done in secret will reward you.* Matthew 6:6

Prayer is talking to God. We associate prayer with bringing before Him our petitions and requests, our needs and supplications.

"A life without prayer is a powerless life", I read in 'Streams in the Desert'. Prayer, I once read, is like the fuel in an engine. We will not get anywhere without it.

David Davis said in *The Elijah Legacy* "Many are powerless because they are prayerless" and "our public ministry will only be as powerful as our private prayer life."

Jesus teaches us by His own prayer life. He often went to be alone with God, getting up early in the morning or praying all night alone with His Father in a solitary place or on a mountain. He said:

> *The Son can do nothing by Himself; He can do only what He sees His Father doing.* John 5:19.

If Jesus could do nothing without the Father, how much more do we need to get alone with God and to be in close communion with Him as Jesus was with His Father. Then the work we are given to do will have depth and power.

A quote from page 119 of *Encouraging Women* by Priscilla Reid:

> E. M. Bounds made the point that Satan trembles even when the weakest Christian prays because he knows that 'they go to fetch strength against him.'

David Hathaway says:

> I want to share a secret with you: you will become what your prayer life is.
>
> Prayer is so important, because it is our relationship with God through the Holy Spirit. The things that God has called you to do are not possible with men. So we have to pray in faith, and it will happen. But if it is not in your heart, it will never happen.

Trusting

In our Ministry we are called to trust God completely. Jesus said to us:

> *"I AM your Provider. I AM Jehovah Jireh."*

He said we are only to ask Him what we need to fulfil our commitments to the Pastors, Fellowships and families. The Holy Spirit will touch hearts to give. We are a faith Ministry depending on the Lord for His Provision. Jesus is called *"Faithful and True"* (Revelation 19:11).

F. B. Meyer reminds us:

> One way or the other, we must learn the difference between trusting in the gift and trusting in the Giver.

> *Sometime later the brook dried up.* (Elijah at the Kerith Ravine, 1 Kings 17:7).

> Whenever our earthly stream or any other outer resource has dried up, it has been allowed so we may learn that our hope and help are in God, who made heaven and earth.

Waiting

Waiting for God and waiting upon Him is crucial to the Ministry. Samuel Dicky Gordon said:

> Waiting – keeping yourself faithful to His leading – this is the secret of strength. And anything that does not align with obedience to Him is a waste of time and energy.

Waiting is a difficult discipline because we always want action, to be doing something now rather than later. But we actually waste our time, rush ahead of God and gain nothing whatsoever, maybe even losing time in our haste.

As we read in "Streams in the Desert":

> Waiting may seem like an easy thing to do, but it is a discipline that a Christian soldier does not learn without years of training.

We are learning to wait upon Him in the Secret Place, to wait for Him:
to open doors
to provide contacts and supporters
to bring the finance needed.

We are learning to walk with God in His Ministry. We don't ask God to walk with us in our ministry. He goes before and He comes behind.

The Lord will go before you, the God of Israel will be your rear guard. Isaiah 52:12.

He is Sovereign. He leads, He guides, He maintains. The work is His. He said: *"I AM the Mount Moriah Trust."*

Thanksgiving & Praise

Throughout the years of Ministry, the Lord has taught us to always praise Him and give thanks whatever the circumstances.

Enter His gates with thanksgiving and His courts with praise; give thanks to Him and praise His Name. Psalm 100:4

Thanksgiving and praise are keys that open the doors of Heaven's storehouses and blessings. They are the keys to open the door into His Presence.

You are worthy, our Lord and God, to receive glory and honour and power. Revelation 4:11.

To Him who sits on the throne and to the Lamb
Be praise and honour and glory and power,
For ever and ever! Amen. Revelation 5:13.

Chapter 11

Our different roles

The Lord has assigned to each his task. 1 Corinthians 3:5

Tony had been faithfully administering the work of the Trust, before he had made a commitment to the Lord by being born again.

But God had been preparing him for many years. I had always shared much of what I learned at Conferences and courses, we read 'Everyday with Jesus' together and all the Bible passages. He often came to Church and loved listening to Lance Lambert when he visited Three Mile Cross. The Lord encouraged me saying that the power of His Word would work in Tony's life. He gave me this scripture:

The Holy Scriptures, which are able to make you wise for salvation through faith in Christ Jesus. 2 Timothy 3:15

Ruth, a very wise and astute believer in the Lord, had watched Tony and said one day that it was as if he was approaching a motorway and would come down the slip road to get on the motorway and gently join the traffic.

I held on to that picture. It was a prophetic word from the Lord because during one of our visits to Israel in 2008 Tony gave his life to the Lord and slipped quietly into God's Kingdom. He was baptised a few days later in the Jordan River by Pastor Claude Ezagouri and

Sasha, the worship leader. Jesus had led Tony to the Galilee, the area of His own Ministry, to draw him to Himself.

Some had been surprised that Tony was doing the Work of God when not yet in the Kingdom, but God is God. He knows the heart, the right time for re-birth. We often try to fit the Almighty God into a box – of our limited ideas and expectations. We want God to do things the way we want and expect. But God will not fit into our plans and schemes; we fit into His. He is so vast and so way above our smallness:

> *As the Heavens are higher than the earth, so are My Ways higher than your ways and My thoughts than your thoughts.*
> Isaiah 55:9

When Beryl Moore saw Tony in 2009 she said that he was "radiant". Ann Wilson a friend and supporter saw him that same year and said she saw "phenomenal growth" in him. God is the Master Architect of our lives!

My precious husband has been gifted by the Lord with a wide range of skills developed during his business career, giving him the perfect background for managing the Trust. He administers the day-to-day running of the Trust and its finances; deals with the requirements of the Charity Commission and Her Majesty's Revenue & Customs (HMRC); prepares our presentations; and organises our travel itineraries and speaking schedules.

Jesus empowers us to do the work He has called us to do. He equips us for the task and gives us everything we need. As the Lord chose and gave the ability to those who worked in the Tabernacle:

> *Then the LORD said to Moses, 'See, I have chosen Bezalel son of Uri, the son of Hur, of the tribe of Judah, and I have filled him with the Spirit of God, with wisdom, with understanding, with knowledge and with all kinds of skills ... Also I have given ability to all the skilled workers to make everything I have commanded you.'* Exodus 31:1-3,6.

God provided a skilled worker in the temple:

> *Huram was filled with wisdom, with understanding and with knowledge to do all kinds of bronze work. He came to King Solomon and did all the work assigned to him.* 1 Kings 7:14

Praise the Lord for filling Tony with His Spirit and for giving him the gifts, abilities and knowledge to do the work of God. God has graciously given him exceptional skills to run and administer the Trust. Tony says that when he looks back on everything he did in his paid working life he can see that it was in preparation for running the Mount Moriah Trust. This even extended to the Lord engineering his early retirement in 2005 so that he could give his full time and attention to the Trust.

Chapter 12

God chooses the workers;
Each one has a role to play

I have chosen you. Isaiah 41:9.

Over the years the Lord has steered and guided us, taught and trained us, arranged Divine appointments, allowed difficulties and challenges to strengthen us.

Early on we were confronted by the Jezebel spirit that tried to destroy the work and bring us down into confusion and despair. I do not feel that it is appropriate to go into detail but suffice to say it was a painful experience. God in His Sovereign Power and Goodness has always brought us through, wiser than before. He has always protected us and His Trust.

Over the years He has given us Trustees, Godly men and women of His choosing, to oversee the work; faithful in their support and wise in their input. Pastor John Angliss, one of the original Board of Trustees, once said the meetings were always so peaceful and orderly. By His Grace, they have always been harmonious and seem to flow in the Power of the Holy Spirit.

The Lord also graced us with Ken Burnett the founder of 'Prayer for Israel' (PFI) as Patron.

During one of my ministry times with Beryl, my spiritual mentor, she believed the Lord was saying that Ken Burnett was to be the Patron. Inwardly, I thought "How can this be? He runs the international ministry of Prayer for Israel. How would he want to be Patron of Mount Moriah Trust as well?"

But a couple of weeks later at church, Pastor John Angliss announced that there was a visiting speaker that morning, Ken Burnett. My heart missed a beat.

After the service Tony and I approached Ken to ask him if he would consider being our Patron. We felt that if the Lord was in this, we only had to ask him and leave the rest to the Lord. We told him about the Trust. He asked if Pastor John was involved and when he learned he was, he said he would pray about it. A week later he rang to say he felt the Lord was telling him to accept. Wow. We had our Patron and God's choice. And so began a lovely relationship with Ken until he died in 2014.

In May 2006 Ken wrote:

I am so glad that the Lord Himself birthed the work into which you have been called. There is a golden thread running through it which I see as of key worth in the Lord's purposes. It may have begun as more of a financial support ministry for the individual, but that personalised support is bringing with it also personalised prayer backing – which is of immeasurable value to the individuals, the couples, the families and the fellowships.

The fact that the Lord is simultaneously calling you into a purer, closer, more intimate (and more costly) relationship with Him – indicates the nature of what He wants to <u>also accomplish in the personal lives of those that your ministry is supporting</u>. You may think that to be awesome! If so, you are perfectly right. My sensing is that He is entrusting you with precious things. In that regard, can I encourage you to seek the Lord as to a few people – say four to six persons – whom you might ask to keep you personally in prayer: for protection, as well as the Preparation and Purification work of the Spirit.

We so valued Ken's mature and Godly wisdom and his invaluable advice, especially in the early days. We followed his advice and sought out a group of prayer warriors to intercede on our behalf. His passionate love for the Lord Jesus Christ and the Word of God shone from Ken and was the foundation of all he said and did. In July 2006 he wrote:

> Shalom be yours in Jesus's Name. Cling to Him more and more closely as you labour for Him. Not only do you need Him but He loves you and desires your fellowship. Amazing? Of course. But everything about Him is amazing – starting with His grace and love! See Romans 11:33.
>
> Thank you for your email. It is a serious but precious thing to pray for you both. The work you are doing is regal, royal work – infinitely precious to Him. Over thirty times in the Word is Israel described as 'His inheritance' – and if you think that you are involved in caring for those who are thus termed – it is awesome. So I pray for your walk with Him – think of that in a literal way, as it were – in fellowship and conversation with Him... like Adam. For your understanding of Himself, more and more (Colossians 2:3; John 17:3); spiritual wisdom and insight as you consider this and that. Faith as you seek His will. Empowerment in prayer – passion is what we need! But a deepening awareness of Who He is – that we all might worship Him in reality. May He free you (and me also) to begin that mounting up as eagles. By the grace of God may these be amongst my prayer for you as He leads."

The Lord truly blessed us in His choice of Patron for the Mount Moriah Trust. We were so privileged to have Ken's deep spiritual teaching and encouragement. Ken did a great deal to spread the word about the Trust among his friends and the supporters of PFI.

In April 2007 he wrote a letter to support the work and encourage groups or Fellowships to pray:

The Mount Moriah Trust began around 2001 – with its main goal to be a channel by which believers could send gifts to individual believers or families in Israel. This is done in great measure through consultation and co-operation through their respective Pastors, etc. (However, donations are also sent to Fellowships.)

The Trust took up much additional work by tending to individuals, and thus (in my opinion) helped to supplement the work of PFI at the time. It continues to support many folk that PFI were involved with. However, the work has been growing well since then – and Arab believers have increasingly been added. Normally, gifts are despatched within one month of receipt by the Trust.

I have been Patron of the Trust from its early days, and have given advice from time to time – while also commending it at Israel ministry meetings that I have taken. Its founders, Tony and Kathy Stewart, are members of John Angliss's church. They have been visiting Israel annually to maintain some form of personal contact with those they support.

I would invite you to support the work in prayer – especially with the spiritual battles that heighten around us in these days – and to especially remember Tony and Kathy on a personal basis. As is needful for all of us in these days, please pray for their personal walk with God, their love of the Word, their hearing from Him.

Tony and Kathy are prepared to travel (at home or abroad) to speak on the work – should you know of interest from a group or Fellowship".

Ken introduced us to Pastors in Israel. Pastor Howard Bass in Beersheva and Pastor Claude Ezagouri in Tiberias were the first Pastors involved with the Trust.Through Ken and Pastor John Angliss we were invited to churches, or prayer groups in the U.K. It was Ken who said in his book, *Why Pray for Israel?*:

It is true that due to the apathetic, lethargic attitude of the Church as a whole, the Lord has been raising 'para-church organisations' to fill the gap (Ezekiel 34:10–11).

Ken described the Trust as one of those 'para-church organisations', to comfort and help the Jewish people. He was so supportive of the work, he sent another letter to his friends and supporters in July 2009:

I have had the privilege of being linked with the Mount Moriah Trust ever since their being founded in 2002. May I introduce them to you in more detail than you may be aware of?

1. The Founders: Tony and Kathy Stewart are members of, and are supported by the sound Church (SORCF: South of Reading Christian Fellowship) that is pastored by John Angliss. John is actually one of the Trustees of MMT. I am the Patron.

2. The Mount Moriah Trust has steadily grown every year since its founding seven years ago. One of its greatest blessings is its ministry to believers in Israel (Arabs and Jews) – mostly on a fairly personal basis.

    I feel that this is through the will of God, as well as the devotion of its founders. The Trust has grown and has very much helped its Israeli recipients and beneficiaries.

3. Since the start, Tony and Kathy have visited Israel every year:
    a. to gain added detail on the needs;
    b. to confirm the allocation and the usage of the gifts sent through the Pastors with whom they work;
    c. to visit and encourage as many Pastors, congregations, and families as possible.

Ken liked our monthly prayer letters – their "accuracy and brevity"; the PowerPoint presentation of which he said "the sharpness of the pictures, and the conciseness of their language surpass all else that I have ever seen. Not only does this foster fine focused prayer but it raises within its watchers and listeners, that heart insight and that understanding – I sense through the aid of the Holy Spirit!

After a very special visit to see him in Kent in 2009, he gave thanks for "the prospering of the work that is of Him and for Him" and said "I feel more bonded in spirit to you than ever... thank You Lord!"

On one occasion Ken spoke prophetically of the Mount Moriah Trust being greater in the latter days than in the former.

'The glory of this present house will be greater than the glory of the former house' says the Lord Almighty. Haggai 2:9

Praise God for Ken and the strong support we had from him in so many ways. We are indebted to the Lord for Ken's input and encouragement over the years. It was one of His Divine appointments beyond our imagining.

When Ken died on 10 January 2014, we wondered whether the Lord would appoint another Patron. Ken was such a special man – who could follow in his footsteps? We prayed about it and left the outcome in His hands.

Later that year in May, we attended the Christian Resources Exhibition at Sandown Park Racecourse in Esher, Surrey. We had a stand to promote the work of the Mount Moriah Trust. We shared the stand with our Trustee Mark Dunman and his wife Margaret. Mark was promoting his book 'Has God Really Finished with Israel?'. I felt very uncomfortable talking about the Trust's work to an unknown audience because of the number of people who expressed very negative thoughts and attitudes towards Israel. The Lord had anointed Tony, Mark and Margaret to speak boldly about Israel, so I stayed at home and prayed for them. However, the Lord said I was to attend the Exhibition on the Thursday of that week.

I was surprised and delighted to learn that David Pawson and David Hathaway were speaking that day. Was the Lord leading us to a new Patron? Was that why He had asked me to attend that day? I was full of expectation and anticipation.

We had met David Hathaway at a conference about a year earlier and he had been delighted to hear that the Lord had established the Mount Moriah Trust as a result of his "Fire Over Jerusalem" conference in Jerusalem in 2001.

As I listened to David Hathaway, the Lord was telling me to approach him after the seminar. I joined the queue to speak with him and asked if he would consider being the Patron of the Mount Moriah Trust. He asked if it was about Israel. I said it was and explained very briefly what we did. Immediately he said, "Yes, he would be Patron". No thinking or praying about it. I stood open-mouthed at how easy the Lord had made it yet again!

I looked so surprised, David said "Where is your faith?" I was just so astounded at the Lord's provision. We had a new Patron; the Lord's choice, in His timing, in His way. I realised that if I had not gone to the Exhibition that day as the Lord had instructed, we would have missed God's opportunity to bring David Hathaway into the work as Patron. How easy it can be to miss God-given opportunities. How many do we miss in our lifetime? We need always to be open and alert to God's promptings if we want all that God has prepared for us.

The Lord had given us such a great man of faith to be the Patron of the Faith Ministry God had birthed. Having read his books about his evangelistic outreaches, the healing miracles and the demonstrations in his life of the Power of God, we were deeply grateful to the Lord for his Patronage.

Amazingly, the work of the Mount Moriah Trust had begun through David's Conference in Jerusalem in 2001 and now in 2014 the Lord had given us David as our Patron.

What an awesome God He is. He knows the end from the beginning.

I AM the Beginning and the End. Revelation 22:13.

Chapter 13

Sharing our material blessings

And let us consider how we may spur one another
on toward love and good deeds. Hebrews 10:24

God's Heart is for the poor and needy. Many times in the Bible we read of His displeasure at His people's failure to help them. God said in Deuteronomy 15:11

> *There will always be poor people in the land. Therefore, I* **command** *you to be open-handed towards your brothers and towards the poor and needy in your land. [Emphasis added]*

He says in Proverbs:

> *He who gives to the poor will lack nothing, but he who closes his eyes to them receives many curses.* Proverbs 28:27.

> *Blessed is he who is kind to the needy.* Proverbs 14:21

> *Whoever is kind to the needy honours God.* Proverbs 14:31

He speaks clearly of our duty to the poor in Isaiah 58:7

> *Is not this the kind of fasting I have chosen …. To share your*

food with the hungry and to provide the poor wanderer with
shelter – when you see the naked, to clothe him...

In Proverbs 19:17, He says:

He who is kind to the poor lends to the Lord, and He will reward
him for what he has done.

In Acts 11:26-29 (NLT) we read of the Christians in Antioch giving
help to the believers in Judea:

It was at Antioch that the believers were first called Christians.
During this time some prophets travelled from Jerusalem to
Antioch. One of them named Agabus stood up in one of the
meetings and predicted by the Spirit that a great famine was
coming upon the entire Roman world. (This was fulfilled during
the reign of Claudius.) So the believers in Antioch decided to
send relief to the brothers and sisters in Judea, everyone giving
as much as they could.

In Romans 15:26 Paul encouraged giving to the poor believers in
Jerusalem:

For Macedonia and Achaia were pleased to make a contribution
for the poor among the saints in Jerusalem.

The Lord gave us Romans 15:27 as a basis for the work of the Mount
Moriah Trust:

For if the Gentiles have shared in the Jews' spiritual blessings,
they owe it to the Jews to share with them their material
blessings.

In gratitude for the spiritual blessings we have received from the Jews, we are to share with them our material blessings. This is a command of God. His commands are to be obeyed. We are called to help those who are in need. The Mount Moriah Trust helps Pastors and the most vulnerable in society:

- the elderly
- the widows
- the Holocaust survivors
- the single mums
- the sick
- the new immigrants
- the alcohol and drug-addicted
- the unemployed
- the children and youth
- the persecuted
- the blind and children with special needs

Because our mandate is to help needy **believers**, we work through Pastors who identify for us those who need help. They are best qualified to monitor the situations. They know when help is no longer needed, when situations change and when the help can be transferred to another.

Some Pastors prefer to have a central pool of money to help with specific needs as they arise, for medical treatment or other emergencies. They are free to use the gifts in what they believe is the best way to help those in need in their Fellowships.

The Adoption Scheme

The Ministry began during the troubled times of the Intifada. We were supporting a few families in Jerusalem and a small number of families in Pastor Claude Ezagouri's Fellowship in Tiberias and Pastor Howard Bass's Fellowship in Beersheva. We felt it would be a good idea to provide "shoulder to shoulder" support by linking UK families with families in Israel. They could then get to know them personally, encourage and support them through prayer and also write or telephone them where possible.

The main obstacle to establishing these relationships was the difficulty posed by the different languages involved, mainly Hebrew, Russian and English. Some in Israel only spoke Hebrew or Russian, some understood English, but had difficulty reading and writing it. The Pastors very kindly helped with the translation of letters. In the UK the only language was English with, maybe, a smattering of Hebrew words although a couple of UK families found Russian-English translators which helped greatly when the letters arrived having bypassed the translator in Israel. Some relationships worked very well and correspondence was achieved despite the difficulties. Some of the UK partners even visited their partner families in Israel.

Some became firm friends and prayer partners. Some were not used to writing letters and there were difficulties. Some are still in touch with each other all these years later.

Rosie, whom I met in Jerusalem at David Hathaway's Conference in 2001, was the first supporter of the Mount Moriah Trust and has been a faithful partner ever since. She adopted Esther in Jerusalem, gave regularly to support her and helped her with her dental needs. On her visit to Israel, she met Esther and they became firm friends. Esther loved Rosie and was uplifted by her visits. Rosie encouraged her in her walk with Yeshua when she experienced difficult times and the friendship bore fruit; Jew and Gentile together in the love of Christ.

Encourage one another and build each other up. 1 Thessalonians 5:11

Pastor Howard Bass in Beersheva had these memories of the scheme:

The individuals or families that you connected from the congregation to particular brothers and/or sisters in the UK was a source of joy to those in need here. They first of all appreciated hearing *personally* from the MMT contacts. Most of the recipients of this grace were Russian speakers who did not know English. There was only one exception. So, I (Howard) would get a call from different ones to help them understand in Hebrew what had been written, and to help them write something back in English. This also blessed me to see the openness of each one on both sides to share aspects of their lives and their prayer requests. When financial support also began to come in (almost from the beginning), that was a total surprise to them, and they were very appreciative. For some of them, this extra bonus provided temporary relief to the small incomes or pensions that they may have had.

One dear, older couple here would often send a sizeable jar of local honey in the mail back to their "partners" and benefactors. I remember that this actually caused some anxiety on the other side, partly because it became a *lot* of honey over time, and also because it was not quite legal to import honey into the UK. Not to mention, what would it have been like had the containers leaked for some reason. Despite asking this dear couple to not send any more honey, and that the recipients were very thankful for what had already been received, this dear couple continued to send more until a "yellow card" was waved. God bless them!

As the Trust started to support more Fellowships, more families and more supporters, it became impossible to extend the scheme any further. The amount of work that it generated both for the Pastors and ourselves would have become an unmanageable burden if we tried to extend it further.

The scheme and corresponding in that way was for a season. A lot of good came out of it. Many in Israel were touched by the love and concern for them by those in the UK who made such an effort to get to know them, help and encourage them, share in their problems and difficulties and in their joys and good times.

The Lord was establishing the Mount Moriah Trust as a personal Ministry. Tony and I would visit every year to see the Pastors, visit the Fellowships, see as many families as we could, visit homes, share meals together, hear about their lives, the good and the bad times, to pray with them, encourage and help where possible.

It was as if the Lord Himself was visiting the families. He once said to us:

> *"As you give one of my brothers or sisters a hug, it is My arms of love around them, My words of comfort to them."*

It is the Lord who touches their lives with His Presence through us, His channels.

Chapter 14

God's Exhortation to help those in need

Therefore, as we have opportunity, let us do good to all people,
especially to those who belong to the family of believers.
Galatians 6:10

Apart from two years, 2016 and 2019, we have visited Israel every year to further the work. Every year we have tried to meet all the pastors, attend as many Congregational services as possible and visit as many families as we could. In the following pages I have provided a synopsis of memorable events, significant moments of change and growth and events that shaped the lives of those living in God's Land. With each Pastor we review the effectiveness of the last twelve months' support and agree who/what we will support for the next twelve months and the level of that support.

I hope the next few paragraphs will give any reader not familiar with Israel a framework to understand the circumstances that I describe in the pages to come.

The second Palestinian Intifada (Uprising) lasted from September 2000 until February 2005 and resulted in the building of the West Bank security barrier to prevent terrorists and suicide bombers from entering the country. During this period a total of 1,137 Israelis were killed of whom 887 (78%) were civilians and 8,341 were injured of whom 5,676 were civilians, 3,000 Palestinians also died. Bombings and suicide bombings in buses, restaurants and markets were commonplace. Tourism, normally a large part of Israel's economy dried up leaving thousands who worked in hotels, restaurants, tour bus companies, airlines, taxis and the supply chain out of work. Much as we dislike the concept of the security barrier it was effective in bringing the killings to an end.

The total population of Israel at the start of 2020 (excluding Gaza and the Palestinian Authority (PA) parts of the West Bank) was 9.1 million made up of 6.7 million Jews, 1.9 million Arabs and 434,000 others. In general, the towns and cities are either Jewish or Arab. Jerusalem has Jewish neighbourhoods and Arab neighbourhoods. Haifa is a notable exception where Jews and Arabs live alongside one another.

Those making Aliyah back to Israel find the first couple of years difficult especially those who are elderly. New arrivals need to learn to speak, read and write Hebrew before they can get a good job – even professionals can only do manual labour until they have requalified in Hebrew. Not only that, there is a big cultural change to adjust to.

The number of Messianic Jews (Jews who believe that Jesus is the Jewish Messiah) has increased from a handful in the early 1960s to around 35,000 in 2020. They suffer harassment and persecution from ultra-Orthodox Jews who refuse to accept that a Jewish believer in Jesus can remain Jewish. They say that they have become Christian and have stopped being a Jew and therefore see all Christians as missionaries trying to change their religion and take away their Jewishness.

There were 161,000 Christian Arabs in Israel when the Trust started, but this has gone down now to around 130,000 due to emigration. Arab believers are harassed and persecuted by the Muslim population and authorities in their towns.

Nothing much has changed for believers in the Holy Land since Jesus and His apostles were there over 2,000 years ago!

Chapter 15

Mount Moriah Trust 2002 – 2005

2002

God has always le us to the Pastors and Leaders He wants us to support. He speaks to us through His chosen channels, through circumstances where we meet Pastors or through word of mouth from one Pastor to another.

Ken Burnett, our Patron, introduced us to Pastor Claude Ezagouri in Tiberias and to Pastor Howard Bass in Beersheva. They were the first Pastors into the work of the Mount Moriah Trust. Ken had explained to them 'who we were' and 'what we did'. They identified the neediest members of their Congregations and we began to help them with regular finance and with prayer.

As we increased the number of needy families and were able to send financial help on a monthly basis, we received letters of thanks:

> What a joy it is that believers in other parts of the world take an interest in the believing community here in Israel. Igor and I are especially grateful that you are taking a special interest in us.
>
> Thank you for your financial gift. It will go to the purchase of schoolbooks for our youngest daughter, Elena. Elena will certainly appreciate your generosity. Igor and Alla

Many parents and single mums struggle to buy schoolbooks for their children. Education is free but the books have to be purchased. If there are a number of children in the family, it can be a huge expenditure to provide the books needed and many children do not have all the books they need.

Dima and Ella Brodkin from the same Fellowship wrote:

> We were so happy for all your concern and attention towards us. Thank God that you found the opportunity to help us and also that your help was really at a time of need. We thank God for you because exactly at this time we didn't have money, and the money that you sent us was used to buy food. We know that God is never late!

We have found this on so many occasions, the money has been so timely, arriving at the greatest moment of need. God sees every need and His timing is perfect!

Our giving brings forth thanks to God which is pleasing to Him:

> *This service that you perform is not only supplying the needs of God's people but is also overflowing in many expressions of thanks to God.* 2 Corinthians 9:12.

The work started with three families in Jerusalem. Shimon and David used the money to fill their refrigerators with food. Not having enough money to buy food was an increasing problem in Israel in 2002.

Esther was a divorced lady with four children, three of whom were in the Military and despite working long hours as a cleaner, she struggled to pay for her basic needs. She had been living without water, electricity and telephone for two weeks. The Trust was able to provide funds to get her essential services restored and her debts restructured. Our friend and co-ordinator, Moshe, helped her to move into cheaper accommodation to reduce her bills.

Pastor Claude Ezagouri from the Morning Star Fellowship in Tiberias commented on life during the intifada:

> Unemployment in the region is more rife and intense than other parts of the Land. I welcome your project to help the needy families. Indeed, this is a time when the difficult situation in Israel plunges more and more families into poverty.

This sentiment was echoed by Pastor Howard Bass from the Beersheva Fellowship:

> There is a great financial burden on many of the believers in the flock due to the state of the economy and to the unrighteousness of many employers. No doubt the Mount Moriah Trust will be of great encouragement to the needy families knowing that God is opening His arms to them in His love through you.

By the end of December 2002, we had extended the Trust's support to eighteen families.

God gave us the logo for the Trust – the loaves and the fish. We are to give out what we have, and our baskets will be replenished. We experienced this time and again. When we sent our gifts to Israel, leaving us little in the account, a cheque would arrive the very next day.

We covenant to give to the pastors and families when we visit them each year, before we have the money to support our giving. We agree how much we will give and what it will be used for and then we trust God to provide. At the end of our visit we have agreed the basis of our next twelve months' expenditure without knowing that we will have the money in the bank. It would be easy to share out the money that we have each month, but the Lord has said we are to trust Him as our Provider for the amounts we have covenanted to give.

Working in this way is a real faith-building exercise. Our dependence on God was increasing daily as we learned to become a Faith Ministry. The Lord has said we are to trust His Holy Spirit to touch hearts to give. Therefore, we do not fundraise or ask people for specific sums of money. We tell them that there are needs without quantifying the amount; we leave the Lord to touch hearts accordingly. We speak about specific amounts only to the Lord.

Little by little the word of the work of the Trust was being taken by individuals to various parts of the country – Devon, Somerset, Lancashire, Berkshire, Oxfordshire, Buckinghamshire, Kent, Suffolk and Northern Ireland. God has said that all that is required of us is to be faithful to Him and what He is doing – we must leave the results to Him. He encourages us to continue in our prayers, our support, our giving for those in need in His Land.

> *Let us not become weary in doing good, for at the proper time*
> *we will reap a harvest if we do not give up.* Galatians 6:9.

One of our Trustees, Rod Wood, gave us a word from the Lord that through the Trust, God is building a motorway. A motorway needs careful preparation and good solid foundations that take time to build but once completed, the traffic will flow quickly along it.

> *My highways will be raised up.* Isaiah 49:11.

Build up, build up, prepare the road! Remove the obstacles out of the way of my people. Isaiah 57:14.

Build up, build up the highway! Isaiah 62:10.

2003

We were supporting twenty families and individuals in Israel by April 2003. Little by little the trust was growing as the foundations were being laid.

Ken Burnett had said to us to walk before we run. Such wise advice. We could be in danger of trying to grow too quickly. We also believed that it would be better to support a smaller number of people with funds that would make a significant difference, rather than give a lesser amount to more people with little or no positive outcome.

The economic situation continued to worsen and affect more Israeli families, but we needed to wait for the Lord to enlarge our territory. God had shown us that prayer and intercession are the fuel for the engine that drives the work of the Trust and without it we will not get very far.

We set in place a number of experienced prayer warriors who were committed to pray for the work. Such a necessary and invaluable part of any ministry.

When we visited Israel in May 2003 the troubles were still ongoing. There was tension throughout the land. Driving from Tiberias to Jerusalem through the Jordan Valley and the West Bank, we were aware, at the various checkpoints, of the unease and mistrust that had been generated by the current situation between Israel and the Palestinians.

Soldiers patrolled with guns poised for trouble whilst cars passed through the checkpoints. Palestinian cars, identifiable by the colour of their licence plates, were given extremely thorough searches.

In Jerusalem we visited Eli and Eitan and their families. These two men had been shot at point blank range by a terrorist as they were working on telephone cables. It was a miracle that they were alive.

Eli was still recovering and needed to attend hospital several times a week. He was in great pain and still had part of a bullet lodged in his stomach. Eitan too still had a bullet lodged inside him which was too difficult to remove. Miraculously he was improving. Both these families needed some financial help until they were able to return to work.

Shimon, who was deaf, caused by not wearing ear-defenders whilst in an artillery unit fighting in the 1982 Lebanon war, lived alone and struggled to make ends meet. He had only a small salary from his part-time job as a security guard and on the day we visited him, his fridge was completely empty. He had no food whatsoever in the apartment so we gave him a gift to go out and purchase food.

Esther, who continued to struggle financially had the added worry of her son, 'K' who needed an operation to correct blindness in his right eye which was the result of an accident in childhood. Praise the Lord, when we came home to the UK a donor provided the money needed for his eye operation.

David, his wife and their children struggled to exist on David's part-time job as a security guard. There was such need and we were deeply moved by the families' circumstances. But God said:

> I will help the families you support in ways you will not know. They are My precious children. Do not grieve over them. I will protect them and draw them closer to Me. I have plans and purposes for all My children. Continue to lift them up in prayer and you will see their salvation. Bless the families, put My arms around them and I will fill them with My Love, My Hope and My Courage.

There were times of great encouragement when we saw improvements through the regular gifts that we had been able to provide. In her difficulties Esther had stopped caring for herself and her appearance, but we noticed she started to look after herself and her appearance and had found someone to share her apartment and the bills. She was much happier and more positive thanks to Yeshua who saw her need.

When we visited Shimon again on his birthday, he had spruced up his apartment and had used the Trust's gift to stock his fridge and buy fruit and a birthday cake to celebrate with us. He had perked up and enjoyed playing host and we absolutely had to eat half of a very large watermelon and his cake! It was good to see his spirit lifted by the help he had received and by something as simple as a visit and some company.

For the first time ever we saw begging on the streets of every town and city that we visited. It was another indication of the poor economic plight of many of the people in Israel at that time.

God showed us earlier in the year what He means by true fasting –

Is it not to share your food with the hungry and to provide the poor wanderer with shelter. When you see the naked, to clothe him... and if you spend yourselves on behalf of the hungry and satisfy the needs of the oppressed then your light will rise in the darkness, and your night will become like the noonday. The Lord will guide you always; He will satisfy your needs in a sun-scorched land and will strengthen your frame, you will be like a well-watered garden, like a spring whose waters never fail.
Isaiah 58:7,10-11.

What promises!

The Trust is totally dependent upon the Lord to provide for every need. We look to Him for the finances needed to fulfil our monthly commitment to the families in Israel through those who support the Trust by giving, praying and helping with the work.

Pastor John Angliss reminded us of George Mueller, the founder of the orphanages in Bristol, and his gift of faith to rely upon the Lord for everything. Throughout his life he never made a request for financial support.

We believe that the Mount Moriah Trust has been called to do the same. We are to believe in God's continuing provision and to come to the Throne of God to receive all that we need.

One of the Trust's unique strengths and something that is greatly appreciated by supporters, is that every penny donated goes directly to the needy families in God's Land. There are no administration or other charges taken out of the money donated by our generous supporters. These costs are all covered privately, similarly all transport and accommodation costs for Trustees' visits to Israel are privately funded.

This is the way the Lord wants us to run the Trust. The work is His and we are to walk in His supernatural provision.

In the Autumn of 2003, the situation was worsening in Israel. There was dire financial hardship. There were husbands committing suicide because they were ashamed that they could not support their families and a teenager committed suicide rather than be a burden on his single parent mother.

The elderly, invalids and single parents had had their benefits cut by 50% and many more soup kitchens had been opened. Teachers had lost their jobs as a result of school budget cuts and children with special needs were particularly affected.

Claude Ezagouri told us that he had families in his Morning Star Fellowship who were in dire financial straits. One widow who could not pay her electricity bill had her electricity cut off. That had never happened to her before.

He said "We are spending much more time trying to help people as their financial situation is very serious now." It was three years since the start of the Intifada and the economic situation was deteriorating.

God's timing for the Mount Moriah Trust to be born was perfect!

We praised God for His care and concern in providing supporters and Claude and the Fellowship praised God that the money so kindly given was making a difference. Claude said that "the money will help them a lot." He often heard the recipients say when the gifts were received, "the timing is perfect!"

Israel seemed poised to enter a new era of violence. Bloodshed on both sides had led to deepening hatred and recrimination.

Quoting from an article in the Daily Telegraph on 8 September 2003, the Hamas terrorist group proclaimed that "the Holy Land was entering the Gates of Hell." They said they had only one goal: "the destruction of Israel and every Jew is a target, marked for death." Against this background of hatred, the Israeli people had to live out their daily lives, with fear and uncertainty a constant factor.

Moshe told us that children were now very fearful because of the rumour that the suicide bombers would soon start to target residential apartment blocks, attacking Israelis in their homes.

The Daily Telegraph on 30 September 2003 carried an article about a recent survey carried out in Israel. The deeply pessimistic opinion poll stated that Israelis are in open despair about their country's future. Two-thirds of those questioned predicted that the Intifada would continue or worsen in the coming year.

Twenty-one percent of parents believed that their children were even more pessimistic than they were. Israel's economy had been in recession for two years and unemployment exceeded ten percent, an austerity budget was being imposed and a public sector strike began on 29 September. Forty-three percent of Israelis believed that their living standards would worsen in the coming year. We gave thanks to God that He had called us, as Gentile believers, to stand with our Jewish brothers and sisters at such a time as this.

Jesus said: *I tell you the truth, whatever you did for one of the least of these brothers of Mine, you did for Me.* Matthew 25:40.

Tony and I spent two weeks in Eilat in November 2003. For years Eilat had provided respite for Israelis and tourists away from the terrorist activities in the rest of the country.

Terrorist attacks in Eilat were almost unheard of but during our stay, there was an incident at the Israel – Jordan Border Post just outside Eilat. A Jordanian who had delivered meat from Amman into

Israel every day for a year, one morning also brought in an AK-47. He opened fire on a group of tourists from Ecuador, killing one woman and injuring four others before being shot and killed. Despite their stoicism it was clearly a shock to the local people who saw the attack as an attempt to reduce even further what little tourism remained in Israel at that time.

When we visited the Tourism Office in Eilat we were presented with a certificate of appreciation for our visit (see pictures).

Every day the Israeli security forces were foiling attempted attacks and bombings throughout the length and breadth of the country. You did not hear about that in the media in the U.K!

Despite these successes some atrocities still happened. During our time in Israel, two soldiers were killed guarding a roadblock on the Bethlehem bypass. One of the soldiers was on the telephone to his mother when he was shot and killed. Two security guards were also murdered in East Jerusalem and Fatah claimed responsibility.

In a European poll fifty-nine percent of Europeans believed that Israel was the largest single threat to world peace and a U.S. pastor had warned that global anti-Semitism was growing at a pace unprecedented in the last half century.

But God was calling Christians to stand with Israel – those believers who understand the importance of Israel in the end time purposes of God.

Jay Rawlings, in his Jerusalem Vistas Newsletter said:

> True believers in Jesus are about the only true friends that Israel has in the entire world. Thank you for who you are, shine friends, keep shining for the Lord, right where you are. Due to the dire straits here, Israelis and Palestinians are all living with painful economic constraints.

We had been called to help our needy Jewish brothers and sisters in Christ. We had been given a mandate to help believers who are finding life difficult in so many ways – the economy, the violence, the isolation and the uncertainty. We were and still are in the Ministry of Encouragement; let us encourage them with our support.

We knew that these things must take place before our Lord Jesus comes again. We needed to continue to stand firm in the Lord, to stand with those believers in Israel who needed help as never before, encouraging them in their one and only hope; their Messiah Yeshua, their Prince of Peace.

God's hope for the people of Israel:

Although you have been forsaken and hated with no-one travelling through, I will make you the everlasting pride and joy of all generations. Isaiah 60:15

No longer will violence be heard in your land, nor ruin or destruction within your borders, but you will call your walls Salvation and your gates Praise. Isaiah 60:18.

2004

By 2004 the situation in Israel was worsening. Moshe, our Jerusalem co-ordinator, reported that since the assassination of Hamas chief, Sheik Ahmed Yassin, the streets of Jerusalem had been deserted. There was great anxiety and fear among the people as they waited for the terrorist reprisals they knew would come. Hamas made a statement saying: "Sharon has opened the gates of hell and nothing will stop us cutting off his head."

America had advised against travelling to Israel and groups were cancelling their trips. Life was getting harder for the people of Israel and by God's grace, we were able to support more families in need.

The Lord reminded us of His Word:

The way we administer this charitable work will bring honour to the Lord. 2 Corinthians 8:19 (CJB).

We received a generous gift of £1,000 from a donor who had been told by the Lord that the money was needed immediately in Israel. We shared the money between the Tiberias and Beersheva Fellowships as an extra gift and received these responses:

> I am so grateful to the Lord and to you for this extra gift! Because of the strike of the Social Services there are so many needs this month that I wondered how we would meet them. Now we have God's answer, praise His Name. Claude Ezagouri.
>
> Every good and perfect gift comes from Our Father in Heaven! God bless you all. Thank you so much for your prayers, gifts and support! Howard Bass.

Trust supporters, Gordon and Barbara Povey, spent ten weeks living in Israel and gave us this report:

> Life in Israel today is not easy, there are so many hurts, not the least the unemployment and poverty. November 2003 statistics showed 680,000 unemployed (10.7% of the population) and 20% of the population living below the poverty line including 618,000 children.
>
> The youth is in need of a great deal of prayer, for many of those who have completed their army service feel that Israel can no longer offer them a future. Around 760,000 Israelis now live permanently abroad and with the ongoing terror are unlikely to return at any time soon.
>
> Children under the age of fifteen need to be supported by much prayer and not be discouraged by words of hopelessness that their parents may utter in the home. Prayer is also needed for the (Christian) labourers in the land for many are waiting for their visas to be renewed. This is not straightforward and many, having had their extensions refused, have been forced to return to their homelands.

However, the Lord is working His purposes out. The Jewish people are more open to receive the Word than we have ever experienced before in these last ten years. They are also ready to receive prayer from Christians and even ask for it.

I know that the Lord… upholds the cause of the needy. Psalm 140:12

We received wonderful words of encouragement from the Lord:

*Come to My storehouses, they are limitless. Be **bold** in your requests, you can never ask too much! It is not greed to seek all that I have, it is faith in Jehovah Jireh. I AM Almighty God, Elohim, El Shaddai, Creator of all things. You can never ask for the impossible because all things are possible for your God. I AM the Eternal, Everlasting One in whom all things begin and end. I AM Everything. If you **know** Me, you have Everything."*

*I have given you a heart to love My people and My Land. You are to serve them, to show them My love; to comfort them; to soften their hearts. I will love them through the work of the Trust. Call on Me as your Provider to supply **all** your needs.*

*I have given you the word 'bold'. Think on this and all that it means. If you **know** you have been called for this purpose, that the work is Mine, that our hearts are together in unity and purpose, then your horizons are limitless. Reach out to me more. The storehouses are vast, they are filled with everything you need to do the work.*

*Let this knowledge go deep into your being, then you will call on Me and I **will** answer. Rejoice and delight in My goodness and loving-kindness.*

Further encouragement came in messages from families who were receiving help, telling us about the difference it was making to their lives:

We are writing to tell you how much we appreciate you helping us. We are a family of eight and the money we earn seems to vanish in thin air – there are so many needs. It is encouraging when people like you want to help. Nadav and Kathy

From Myriam:

To Mount Moriah – Personal Shalom!

My name is Myriam and I want to thank you for the great help to me and my family. I'm especially encouraged by your good testimony (by your help) to the people of God in Israel.

I want to thank you also for your prayers and intercession and the love of Yeshua to me and my family and my brothers and sisters in Israel. You are a great help to us in these difficult moments. I would like to ask you please to continue to pray for us, for my daughter 'L', she is a backslider, but I believe the Lord in His mercy and grace will bring His daughter back to Him, her first love. I ask also for prayers for me for health and deliverance and for the economic situation now. Please pray for the peace of Jerusalem and her salvation, and for the Morning Star believers, for their deliverance and growing that the Lord will raise more evangelists in our midst.

May the Lord God of Israel abundantly bless you all and use you in wonderful ways to fulfil His will in the earth.

Yours in the love of the Messiah Yeshua,

Your sister, Myriam.

An extract from Yardena's letter:

I am twenty-three years old and I have been unemployed for four years. The money I received this month went to pay rent, electricity, water and gas… Thank you so much for your support.

Not one of all the Lord's good promises to the House of Israel failed; every one was fulfilled. Joshua 21:45

Pastor Howard Bass sent a message to all the supporters of the Mount Moriah Trust:

Shalom Kathy and Tony,

Randi and I want to thank the Mount Moriah Trust for its trustworthiness in handling the stewardship which you have received from God to bless families in the Body of Messiah in Israel. We want to especially express our appreciation for the Trust's prayers, communications and financial gifts to several of our families in the Nachalat Yeshua Messianic Congregation in Beersheva.

We have just heard the news this week that there are almost 1.5 million Israelis living in poverty, nearly half of them children. Next year's report (regarding 2004) is expected to be grimmer. The saints – the believers in Jesus as Lord and Messiah – are not exempt from this hardship, as you are all well aware of even in the U.K. Your love and generosity towards the supported families and individuals is of great encouragement to them of our Father's love through their brothers and sisters from faraway lands, which is a wonder in itself.

May the Holy Spirit continue to lead you in ways to honour the Lord Jesus Christ and to be a blessing to others, including the poor saints in Israel. (Romans 15:26-27).

God bless you and your service for His sake and the Gospel's. Howard and Randi Bass.

Pastor Claude Ezagouri also sent this message to the supporters:

Dear Tony and Kathy,

For the last two years the economic situation in Israel has

become very difficult and the body of Messiah has been largely affected. The relief that Mount Moriah has brought to several families in our congregation has been extremely valuable. For most of these people it really means having bread on the table and we are grateful to the Lord for the precious help.

The Lord bless you abundantly. Claude and Michelle Ezagouri.

Will not the Judge of all the earth do right. Genesis 18:25

Lena, a widow in her seventies in Pastor Claude's Fellowship, had made Aliyah to Israel six years ago from Russia with her husband and son. Lena's husband was Jewish but Lena is not, this was not a problem when they made Aliyah together. But when her husband died the government said that as she was not Jewish she should return back to her home land and she was being threatened with deportation. She had been unsuccessful with her application for citizenship even though her son is Jewish through his father.

Whilst out shopping in Tiberias Lena was arrested and threatened with deportation back to Russia within a month. Her son had to find $3,000 bail to get her released pending an appeal. To make matters worse, the bank was selling the house they lived in so they would soon have nowhere to live.

During our September visit to Israel we met the families that we were supporting in Jerusalem. Esther was continuing to make good progress. She had moved into a smaller apartment sharing with another believer. They shared the rent and the bills which made a big difference. Esther had a lot of work cleaning people's houses, leaving home at 6:00 AM and not returning some days till 8:00 PM. She was tired but much happier, even though her income was small. With money from her work and the Trust's help she was paying off her debts and would soon receive further support when her son who had just left the Military, found a job.

Shimon was not doing so well and was a little depressed. His hearing aids were not functioning and he had lost his taxi driving job. He had taken customers to the wrong place on a number of occasions and gone to the wrong place to pick people up! His security work had also reduced for the same reason. We decided to buy him new digital hearing aids which we hoped would restore his confidence and transform his life.

David was in a terrible state when we saw him. His marriage had gone very badly wrong and his wife, a non-believer, had thrown him and their two sons out of their house. He had found a cheap apartment and when we visited them they were in a very cold room with just one bed in which they all slept. He had little work, only a few hours as a security guard each day. To add to his misery, he had very bad teeth and gums and was unable to chew food and he was surviving mainly on soup. His dentist quoted NIS 30,000 (almost £4,000) to do the work; He did not earn that much in a year! After some time, David's wife did take him and the boys back into their home.

Eitan had still not fully recovered from the shooting and suffered from nightmares. His two middle sons were traumatised by their father being shot and it was having an adverse effect on their schooling. He was able to work part-time. Eli was making good progress but still attended hospital every week for therapy.

2005

Enlarge the place of your tent. Isaiah 54:2

The year 2005 marked a significant step change for the Trust. After three years of supporting Jewish families *"first for the Jew, then for the Gentile"* (Romans 1:16) whilst at home in the UK, prior to making our annual visit, the Lord said: *"It is time to help your Arab brothers and sisters."*

His purpose was to create in Himself one new man out of the two. Ephesians 2:15.

Up until then we had assumed that the ministry was to be to Jewish believers only but that was about to change as the Lord told us to expand the ministry to Arab Christians in Israel. At that time there were approximately 160,000 Arab Christians of all denominations in Israel itself not counting Gaza or the West Bank.

When we visited Israel later in the year the Lord led us to Pastor Anis Barhoum and his wife, Nawal who ran the House of Light Social Aid Ministry in Shefar'am, an Arab town not far from Haifa. Anis was also the Christian Prison Minister who visited prisons throughout Israel to meet and counsel non-Jewish prisoners.

On the day that we were due to visit Anis & Nawal I was feeling very unwell with a heavy cold so Tony and Moshe drove up from Jerusalem without me. They were very late back that evening as their journey home had been disrupted by the aftermath of a suicide bombing at a market in Hadera where five people were killed and fifty-five injured. The police had set up roadblocks on every intersection from Hadera back to the West Bank in an effort to catch the bomber's accomplices.

Anis and Nawal explained the work of the House of Light and Anis' prison ministry to Tony. They told him about the very needy families that they help and how the Arab believers suffer discrimination and persecution from Muslim family members and the wider Muslim community. In their house they had four rooms where vulnerable individuals, often women, could find refuge.

They told us about Aida, a single woman aged forty-two who had diabetes. She had already lost one leg and one eye to the disease and was in danger of losing the second leg. She was in hospital at the time of the visit. She needed a lot of regular medication and help to pay for transport to and from the doctor and hospital. This was a big expense which she could not afford. If she did not have the money for the transport she could not go for treatment even if she needed it urgently. We agreed that the Trust would provide funds to help Aida.

The second new Christian Arab Pastor that we visited was Pastor Nizar Touma and his wife, Katy, who lead the Church of the Nazarene in Nazareth. We heard about their congregation, their challenges and their needs. The Church ran a pre-school attended by children from both Christian and Muslim families. Muslim families had no problem sending their children to a Christian school; they said the children were taught love and respect which was not always the case at other schools.

From these two visits we learned a lot about the plight of Arab Christians, the problems within the Arab population, the Arab culture and the drug and alcohol problems that affected so many. We could see that there were many needy families and we made agreements to begin to help some of the neediest.

Yad L'Achim, the Jewish counter missionary organisation and the ultra-Orthodox Jews have always stirred up trouble for the believers. Pastor Yoyakim Figueras sent out an urgent prayer request following a campaign in Arad against the members of the Fellowship. The Ultra-Orthodox put up posters in the town warning of "this dangerous sect of Messianic Jews" and showing photographs of members of the Fellowship, including a twelve-year-old orphan girl and a sixteen-year-old boy. His wife Debbie was one of their targets – she was described as a 'dangerous missionary.'

As Yoyakim said "This is a very dirty game and they really need our prayers at this time, especially for the young girl."

You are my hiding place, You will protect me from trouble.
Psalm 32:7

Whilst visiting Pastor Claude and Michelle Ezagouri at the Morning Star Fellowship in Tiberias they told us about a couple from a Druze background. They had a son (ten) and a daughter (eight). When the husband came to the Lord, his family threatened him and attacked him verbally. As a result of the pressure and shock, he had been in Safed Hospital for three weeks. He was diagnosed with having a chemical imbalance that caused him to faint and fall down when under pressure. He had recently lost his job and the family were in debt with a large mortgage to pay – they had nothing to live on. We could not cover all their needs but we agreed to provide Claude with a regular amount to help the family.

Before our visit to Israel the Lord had told us:

> to extend the boundaries of the Trust's work and do not hold back.

> He said, "I AM the Trust and its work. My purposes never fail and you (the administrators) are not to be afraid of taking on greater commitments to help more families. I will provide the supporters and all that is needed."

> Move on the Lord said (Exodus 14:15).

The Lord clearly told us before we went that He had arranged our time in Israel and that we were to visit not only Arab Pastors but also Ethiopian Pastors as there was great need in the Ethiopian communities.

> The Lord will go before you, the God of Israel will be your rearguard. Isaiah 52:12

We met Ken Burnett's friends Mehertie and Emabet Raday, an Ethiopian Pastor and Evangelist at his home in Yavne to explain the Trust's work and to seek ways to help believers in the Ethiopian community. Emabet cooked us a delicious Ethiopian spicy chicken meal and introduced us to Teff which when prepared is grey and looks like a cross between a pancake and a crumpet. It is made from the seeds of the lovegrass plant, is full of minerals and protein and is a staple of the Ethiopian diet. We have to admit it is a bit of an acquired taste but it was a great meal!

Ethiopians at that time, were at the bottom of the social and economic ladder in Israel and were suffering widespread discrimination and persecution. The Ethiopian believers had to endure a lot of persecution and harassment including from within the Ethiopian community itself. As soon as it had become known that Emabet was a believer, she lost her job as a social worker.

Mehertie contacted other pastors and we were led to Pastor Tal Shiferaw and his Messianic Congregation in Jerusalem. We discovered that Pastor Tal, his wife Tigi and their two young boys were living in an apartment which had broken windows leaving the family open to the elements in the cold of winter. The boys were sleeping on the floor as they did not have beds. The family had severe financial problems and Tigi worked three jobs to feed the family and allow Tal to be a full-time pastor.

When we made this need known, the Lord touched hearts to help Pastor Tal. We were able to provide the funds needed to fix the windows and purchase beds and bedding for the boys. From that time on, we have supported Tal and Tigi, as well as four other families in the congregation. There was so much need within the Fellowship.

Chapter 16

Mount Moriah Trust 2006 – 2009

2006

The Israeli economy had been severely hit by the 2006 war in Lebanon. Normal business life in the north had been disrupted by rocket attacks and the whole nation was affected by the call-up of reservists. We thanked God for the safety and protection from rockets of the families in Haifa and Tiberias and praised Him for the miracles that were witnessed – a rocket narrowly missed the home of Pastor Claude & Michelle Ezagouri. Another family living in Haifa was saved when a rocket hit the street not far from where they were standing.

Tourism, on which so much depended, had once again collapsed. Tour groups had cancelled and it would be many months before confidence returned and tours restarted. As a result, there were fewer jobs in shops, cafes, restaurants, hotels and tourism related activities such as tour guides, bus drivers etc.

There would undoubtedly be more believers in need of the Trust's support as a result of this war. We knew already that things had become even harder than they already were for some of the families that the Trust supported.

Pastor David Davis wrote this letter to us:

> Gregory (Grisha), a Jewish immigrant from Siberia came
> to us in a desperate condition over eight years ago. He was

homeless and addicted to heroin. His wife and child left him and went back to Siberia to one of the remote villages where Stalin had banished many Jews. Gregory received the Lord and was fully restored at House of Victory. His wife returned, they were reconciled and now have a second child.

Gregory is a very productive staff member at House of Victory working on a minimal part-time salary. We are praying that the Lord will provide a full-time salary for him enough to support his wife and children. Would The Moriah Trust prayerfully consider sending the House of Victory assistance designated toward his salary?

It is a pleasure to co-labour with you in the Lord's harvest field here in Israel.

With shalom,

Pastor David Davis

The Trust undertook to provide a monthly contribution towards a salary for Grisha so that he could work full time.

We were greatly assisted by Pastor David Davis of Kehilat HaCarmel in setting up support for Ethiopian families in Haifa under Pastor Zechariah Arni. In 2005 Zechariah had lost his job as a High School teacher when it had become known that he was a believer in Yeshua. We discovered that there were many needy families in his congregation and agreed to provide funds for food parcels.

By this time, we were sponsoring thirty food parcels every month for Pastor Tal's congregation in Jerusalem and had doubled the support we were providing to the House of Light.

In October 2002, Pastor Hani Billan from Cana Baptist Church had come to speak at South of Reading Christian Fellowship. As he told us of the needs of his church, I felt that the Lord was saying: *"Pastor Hani is one of the Pastors you will be helping."* Now in 2006, we went to Cana to see him and his wife Shifa to hear more about the church and congregation, the challenges for Christians in this Arab, mainly Muslim, town and discuss how we might help the poor and needy.

Through Pastor Howard Bass, the Lord led us to another new Arab Christian congregation in Bethlehem. We met Pastor Nihad and Salwa Salman at Immanuel Evangelical Church and learned about the challenges for Christians in the town of our Lord's birth. The Christian population of the town that had once accounted for 70% of the population was in rapid decline and Bethlehem was now a difficult place for Christians to live. We committed to helping those in need.

We visited poor and needy families with Pastor Nizar Touma from the Church of the Nazarene in Nazareth. We always remember visiting David and Kamilia with their four children. David was a tiler by profession, but had suffered a terrible injury to his ankle in an accident and was unable to work. They were struggling to cope and they were depressed and anxious. We listened to their worries and concerns and together we prayed with them. The Trust started to help them financially through this difficult period.

By the time we left Israel we were committed to helping around one hundred families across the Land. The Lord richly rewarded the step of faith that we made to extend the scope of the Trust's work. He provided more supporters and more finance and we were able to increase the size of gifts and extend support to additional families.

2007

By the time of the Trust's fifth birthday in May 2007, a lot had been achieved – but there was so much more to do!

> *God... will not forget your work and the love you have shown*
> *Him as you have helped His people and continue to help them.*
> Hebrews 6:10

2007 was the year that Hamas came to power in Gaza. Israel had forceably withdrawn all Jews from Gaza in 2005 in an attempt to trade land for peace in the region. In 2007 Hamas was elected to become the governing body.

115

This was another significant year in the development of the Trust because the Lord told us that it was the time to expand the work further to include Christians in Gaza and Judea and Samaria (the West Bank). He told us specifically that we were to meet and help Pastor Hanna Massad, the Pastor of Gaza Baptist Church in Gaza City.

Despite the intensity of the political situation the Lord said: *"You are not to be political."* He was calling us into His heart, not into politics.

When we arrived in Israel we were told that we could not go into Gaza, it would be unsafe and unwise and it was very unlikely that we would get a permit for a visit. We said: "Lord, it is over to you how we meet with Hanna."

On the following Sunday, we were in Bethlehem attending the service at Immanuel Evangelical Church. Pastor Nihad Salman announced that they had visitors that day and for a moment we thought he meant us, but no, he was talking about Pastor Hanna Massad and a number of families from Gaza. Tony and I looked at each other in amazement. We could not go to Gaza, but the Lord had brought Pastor Hanna to us!

God will always provide a way for His purposes to be fulfilled. Nothing is too difficult or impossible for Him.

I AM the Lord, the God of all mankind. Is anything too hard for Me? Jeremiah 32:27.

These families were in Bethlehem because of the desperate situation in Gaza. Rami, the Christian bookshop manager had been tortured and murdered by Hamas and the Israeli government had allowed some Christian families, including Rami's pregnant wife and children, to leave and come into the West Bank for respite from the atrocities being committed in Gaza.

After the service, we met with Pastor Hanna, his wife Suhad and their two girls and offered to help the needy families in Gaza

Baptist Church who were struggling in a very difficult and dangerous situation. So began a long relationship with Pastor Hanna and a commitment to help the poor and needy in the Gaza Baptist Church. We were all touched by the goodness and mercy of God, who brought us together for good in the midst of tragic circumstances.

After we had returned to the UK, we received the following message from Pastor Hanna Massad:

> Things are fine in the West Bank, but in Gaza it is very, very bad – the worst, never has it been like this! Many children cannot go to school because there is no petrol for the buses or cars which pick them up. Certain vaccines are not available for children.
>
> Fishermen are not able to fish with their boats because they have no petrol. Hamas are refusing to allow one million litres of fuel to be distributed from storage tanks.
>
> We are helping families in Gaza with food and other help.

Whilst we were in Jerusalem we visited Eitan again. He still had a bullet lodged in his body from the terrorist shooting in 2002 and just before Passover, he had sustained terrible injuries in an accident at work. His legs had become trapped in the telephone cable that he was laying. The cable had been attached to a vehicle that then drove off down the street and he was dragged behind the vehicle for fifty or sixty metres. He had broken both legs and the cables had cut his flesh to the bone. He was a big man, and we prayed that he would be able to walk again once his broken legs were healed.

Pastor Nizar Touma of the Church of the Nazarene in Nazareth took us to see David and Kamilia and it was wonderful to see that the Lord was raising them up from the despair and depression that we had witnessed the previous year. David had had an operation on his ankle and although it was not completely right he was able to do a little work. The family were now in a much better place and it was a joy to see that the Lord was lifting them out of their dire situation.

Pastor Hani Billan in Cana wrote to us after we had visited:

To our beloved brethren

We would love to thank you for your honest love and rich giving, for we are truly blessed every time you give us those gifts. What is greater than that is that we notice how the Lord is working through us in our ministry in a powerful way, because we have you, such faithful brethren who lift us and the ministry up in prayers.

Please pray for the ministry in Cana, for us as a family; for the home cells ministry; for the youth meetings and the Sunday School.

The land adjoining the church is for sale. Please pray that the Lord will provide the money for us to purchase it. It will enable us to extend the ministry and the church. We are very afraid that Muslims will buy it and start Islamic activities there.

Finally, please pray for the political situation here so that true peace fills the whole land."

At this time the Lord gave us the following message to give to the Trust's supporters:

Jesus said: *"Come and join Me in what I AM doing. Come and help your brothers and sisters. Pray for them, stand alongside them, encourage them, give to them, help them in their need."*

Truly I tell you, whatever you did for one of the least of these brothers and sisters of mine, you did for me. Matthew 25:40.

God also gave Tony and I this personal message telling us that He was fulfilling His Word:

*Enlarge the place of your tent… you **will** spread out to the right and to the left."* Isaiah 54:2-3. [Emphasis added]

2008

In the Autumn we visited the Land and toured the country meeting all the pastors, reviewing the effectiveness of our support and agreeing how and who or what we would help for the next twelve months. It was mainly a year of consolidation.

The Ultra-Orthodox Gur Hasidim had stepped up their harassment of the believers. They were outside Pastor Yoyakim Figueras' house in Arad at 5:00AM. on their prayer mornings. They had also been approaching and speaking to children of believers' families who innocently gave out family and school details. The Gur had then gone to schools to pressure them into having children removed and to parent's workplaces seeking to force their employer to sack them.

When we attended the service at the Church of the Nazarene in Nazareth we met David and Kamilia again. We hardly recognised Kamilia at first as the change in her was so dramatic and she looked so lovely and vibrant; she had taken care of her appearance and her beaming smile spoke volumes. What a transformation! David was also looking good. He had undergone reconstruction surgery on his badly damaged ankle and after a period of recovery he was now able to work two or three days a week. In 2006 they were in despair but now they were thriving, full of hope and paying off their debts. God had lifted them out of their poverty and into His bounteous goodness. How encouraging it was to see!

Pastor Nizar also took us to see Adel and his wife Mona. Adel was having chemotherapy for a brain tumour, which had affected his spine, leaving him unable to walk without a frame, and he now had very brittle bones. He could not manage the sixty steps to their top floor apartment, making him housebound. If he needed to go to hospital for treatment he had to be carried down all those steps. He also had great difficulty reading and had been given a 'talking Bible'. Mona had given up work to become his full-time carer. We arranged to provide some regular finance to help them. It was a very sad situation for both of them. What a blessing that they knew and loved Jesus.

During our time with Anis and Nawal Barhoum at the House of Light we visited a new family that needed the Trust's help. Yvonne's husband, Gerius, worked, but after paying the rent and utility bills, there was little or no money left for food. Because of their poor diet, the two children aged three and nine months were not very healthy. Yvonne was overwhelmed and the house was a mess. Following the visit, we agreed to assist Anis and Nawal to provide regular meat and vegetables to improve the family's diet.

During our visit to the pastors, fellowships and families it had been a privilege to encourage them and be encouraged ourselves by what the Lord had been doing through MMT. So many of the families had been blessed during the year and they were so thankful to everyone for their prayers and generosity.

On this visit we found that so many of the Pastors were under pressure. Some were dealing with hurtful splits and divisions, others were facing increased harassment and others had difficult financial pressures.

2009

Cana Baptist Church is located very close to the Wedding Church where visitors come to celebrate Jesus' first miracle of turning water into wine. Everyday Pastor Hani Billan watches hundreds of buses and thousands of tourists passing the entrance to his church. He lamented to us the fact that none of these tourists ever came to his church to encourage and pray with today's Christians in the Holy Land. We were extremely touched by this and from that time on, wherever we speak, we have encouraged tours and individual tourists to visit, pray with and encourage the "living stones" throughout the Holy Land. Some very special and lasting relationships with Messianic and Arab pastors and congregations including Pastor Hani and Cana Baptist Church have resulted from these visits.

In Tiberias, Lena an elderly widow had been forced to move into a small apartment which had only a bed, a chair and a camping gas stove. She had no income at all. We worked with Pastor Claude Ezagouri to provide a refrigerator, washing machine, microwave oven and a table. Lena was and still is a dedicated intercessor for Israel, interceding for hours in prayer shifts. Our prayer partners had long prayed that the Lord would act mightily for her and that she would soon receive her citizenship and the benefits that came with it.

Whilst visiting Pastor Howard and Randi Bass we were staying in a hotel in Beersheva and as we went for breakfast one morning, there in the restaurant were Tom Hess and a group of pastors having a breakfast prayer meeting. Pastor Howard introduced us to everyone, explaining why were in Israel and what we did.

After their meeting finished, Pastor Israel Pochtar came up to ask if we could help Kehilat Beit Hallel in Ashdod and we arranged to visit him a few days later.

He organised much needed humanitarian help to the poor Russian families living in the town, but he had not considered whether there were those in his Fellowship who also needed assistance. God knew that there were some who would be glad of help. There were three Beit Hallel congregations in Ashdod, Kiryat Gat, and Ramla with many needy families including the elderly, widows, single mothers and young parents with children. We worked with him on a programme that would provide medicines and food parcels. So began a long-standing relationship with Pastor Israel and Kehilat Beit Hallel.

In November 2009 we met a very remarkable man named Gabriel and his partner Daruka in Jerusalem. Gabriel from South Sudan told us his amazing story of how he fled the civil war in Sudan between the Muslims in the north and the Christians in the south. In 1987 Muslims from the North attacked his village and killed many people including his father and other relatives. In 1989, aged nine, he ran away with a group of other children and spent years criss-crossing Africa travelling on foot to Ethiopia, Kenya, Tanzania and Zambia. They killed wild animals to survive.

With help from Christians he was released from prison in Zambia and moved to a refugee camp. at the age of fifteen. He was able to attend a boarding school between 1997 and 2001 and complete his education. In 2001 with the help of the UN he went back to Kenya and from there went to his home village in Sudan where he found his mother. Militia found him there and accused him of being a rebel and he was sent to the North and put in a camp. Christians managed to get him released and got him a passport.

In 2004 he went to Egypt and was finally accepted as a genuine refugee by the United Nations and he got work in the UN offices as an interpreter. However, the Egyptians made life very difficult for the refugees and in June 2006 he and a friend decided to go to Israel. They paid some Bedouins to get them through Egypt up to the Israeli border. At that time, Egypt would try to shoot anyone trying to get up to the border. The Bedouins had reassured him that if he could get to the border fence he would be well treated by the Israelis. The Bedouins left them some way away from the border and told them to run if the Egyptians saw them and started firing.

The Haaretz newspaper reported that up to fifty refugees each night were crossing from Sinai to Israel and in the span of a month and a half seven hundred Africans had arrived in Israel. At one time Israel had in the country around 40,000 African refugees mainly from Sudan and Eritrea and mainly Christians.

Although Israel treated the refugees well on arrival, they did not give them official refugee status. This meant that they could not officially work, and they had no benefits and no access to free medical treatment. To feed themselves they worked in the black economy – restaurants, cleaning and building sites for cash.

Gabriel made it! He was put in an Israeli prison for a year where he was well treated. In 2008 he was released and went to Eilat and worked in a hotel for six months. He came from a farming background and he longed to study agriculture and go back to farming. He moved to Jerusalem and got a gardening job with a wealthy family. They were so moved by his story that they paid his university fees so that he could do his studies.

This is when we met him and Daruka in their tiny apartment that had no windows. The landlord had divided one room into two tiny apartments giving the apartment next door the only window. The room was just big enough to get a double bed in with half a metre spare to walk past it. At the foot of the bed there was just enough room for a washbasin and toilet behind a curtain on one side and a small table, some shelves and a camping gas stove on the other. To get light and air into the room they had to open the door. The little money Gabriel got from his gardening job was not enough to cover his exorbitant rent of 2,200 shekels (approx. £390) per month, and for food.

Daruka was ill in bed in great pain, she looked very sick and undernourished. She had been ill for some time, but they had no money to pay for an appointment with a doctor. She was so unwell that MMT paid for a doctor to go and visit her in the apartment after we left and for the medicines that she needed.

The absolute minimum that they needed to live on was more than 3,000 Shekels a month so we pledged to help them on a monthly basis and cover further medical expenses. Praise the Lord, Daruka did eventually make a full recovery.

It was a divine appointment meeting Gabriel and Daruka and it was an honour and a privilege to help and support them. He was a man of faith and love and had absolute trust in God. The Lord had miraculously provided for him throughout his extensive journeys through Africa and into Israel. We entrusted Gabriel and Daruka into the care of their Lord and Saviour. They knew their God:

The eternal God is your refuge, and underneath are the everlasting arms. Deuteronomy 33:27

Sometime later, the Israeli government gave them some money and repatriated them to Southern Sudan. We lost touch with them and can only pray that they were able to settle back into Sudan safely and that Gabriel has been able to fulfil his dream of becoming a farmer. If you would like to read more about Gabriel's amazing story and that of others who escaped from Sudan to Israel we recommend Judith Galblum Pex's book: *A People Tall and Smooth.*

Our time in Israel in the autumn of 2009 revealed the need to help more single parent families and Christian refugees. We saw for ourselves the desperate situation that many single mothers found themselves in. Their social welfare benefits were insufficient to cover food, rent and utility bills let alone workbooks for those children that are at school.

Refugees from Sudan and Eritrea were a big problem for Israel. There were over two thousand, mainly Sudanese refugees, in holding camps near the Egyptian border on top of those already in the community. The Lord gave us clear indications that the Trust was to help some of these people.

Chapter 17

Mount Moriah Trust 2010 – 2013

2010

We had decided towards the end of 2009 that it would be a good investment to commission a DVD featuring the pastors with whom we work. We wanted them to personally explain their challenges and tell supporters how the Trust was helping them. Being able to show these videos would be so much more powerful than the audience hearing it from us. It would also have the benefit of putting pastors' faces to names and showing what the country is like to people who have never visited it.

We commissioned Jay Rawlings and his team at Jerusalem Vistas in Jerusalem and briefed the Pastors. The plan was to get as much filming as possible done in advance of our visit in April 2010 so that by the time we were in the country we could sit down with Jay to do the final editing. Jay did a wonderful job, we had so much great material that we decided to split the DVD into two parts so that they would not be too long.

The Lord had given us the the title "The Heart of God" and when completed we had two thirteen-minute DVDs. These DVDs are available to watch today under the videos tab on our website: mountmoriah.org.uk

What valuable and effective tools these DVDs are. We have used them extensively in our presentations to churches and prayer groups ever since and they have contributed greatly to making our presentations interesting and informative.

Poverty was the biggest danger facing Israel according to Welfare and Social Services Minister Isaac Herzog. The Annual Poverty Report published in 2010 showed a 7.5% increase in the number of people living below the poverty line. Those newly reduced to poverty included many single parents, new immigrants and working-class Israelis who had lost their jobs or been forced by their employers to accept significantly reduced salaries.

Wherever we went pastors talked to us about the plight of single mothers and their children. Many children exhibited the symptoms of being in dysfunctional families and the lack of a father figure made the mothers' task of bringing them up even more difficult.

The Lord led us to extend the Trust's support to two new Fellowships. Firstly, we agreed to contribute to Pastor Tony Sperandeo's *widows and orphans* fund that helps over twenty single mothers in the Kehilat HaMaayan congregation in Kfar Saba. A needy young woman whom we had known and helped for some time had recently joined the congregation. She was finding it a struggle coping with work because of her failing hearing aids. We arranged for her to be fitted with digital hearing aids in the hope that these would improve her quality of life.

The second new Fellowship was King of Kings in Jerusalem. We met Sandy Shoshani the National Director of Be'ad Chaim, the pro-life organisation, and her husband Pastor Oded Shoshani who pastors the King of Kings Hebrew speaking congregation in Jerusalem.

Israel has a shocking record on abortion – more children have died through abortion than were killed in the Holocaust. A child can be aborted at any time before the umbilical cord is cut. At the time of writing, there are 20,000 legal abortions and 20-30,000 illegal abortions every year in Israel.

Be'ad Chaim provides counselling for pregnant women and material assistance for the baby in its first year of life. By 2020 it had saved over 2,000 babies from abortion. We provided Sandy with a gift to help in her wonderful work and agreed that we would support some single mothers in Oded's congregation.

We visited an Arab Christian lady in a town in the North with Anis and Nawal Barhoum from the House of Light. She had six children but very little to live on. The week before we saw her, she had been baptised in the Jordan River at Yardenit. Their apartment had three rooms, plaster was falling off the walls, there were no interior doors and there were bare live electric cables poking out of the wall. They only had two chairs between them for sitting at the small table to eat. We took them some groceries and other essentials that the Trust funded and the next day bought them another six chairs (stacking plastic chairs because of the space), a cupboard and two small tables for the children to be able to do their homework. They were an extremely poor but loving family and the mother was sustained by the love of the Lord.

During this visit the Lord spoke to us a lot about the refugees from Sudan and Eritrea that are seeking asylum in Israel. They were mainly from Christian backgrounds. We went with Anis and Nawal to visit a group of Eritrean youths in a holding centre in Hadera who were being prepared for release into the community. We spent two hours with them and enjoyed a time of praise and worship. House of Light had arranged New Testaments in Tigrit (the Eritrean language) for them, small parcels of snacks and a new pair of jeans for each of them. A few days later we visited Pastor Zechariah Arni in Haifa and found that he and his congregation were already providing accommodation and food parcels for twenty adult male Eritrean refugees.

More pastors were using food parcels and coupons that could be used in supermarkets to ensure that the neediest families had the basics. The Trust again increased the number of food parcels that it was funding. Other common needs included medicines/medical care and school workbooks.

Persecution and harassment were increasing and pastors were even receiving death threats. Pastor Nihad Salman in Bethlehem had received such threats and, as a warning of what could happen, unlit Molotov cocktails had been left on the doorstep of his church.

He received threatening phone calls accusing him of brainwashing Muslim background believers (MBBs) who attended his church. He asked us to be very careful what we publish, especially on the website, as these were very sensitive times and there were those who would react aggressively to any misplaced word.

The Hasdey Yeshua Fellowship in Arad was having difficulty opening a bank account, because the local banks were worried about the reaction of the Ultra-Orthodox if they found out that they had agreed to open an account for them.

Life for Pastors and all believers was tough at this time!

2011

Whenever we visit Israel the Lord brings to us new pastors and families that He wants MMT to help. At other times He brings new families to our attention through letters and emails from the pastors. One such e-mail came in from Pastor Claude Ezagouri of the Morning Star Fellowship in Tiberias which led to us substantially increasing the Trust's support for a Druze-Arab member of the congregation:

> Yesterday I went to visit 'S' after it came to my knowledge that he was in utter despair. Apparently the Druze gave the word to people in the village not to buy in his clothes shop because he is a believer. For the last two weeks his sales dropped to almost nothing and he said he felt darkness upon him. We will of course need to check if this situation goes on, but I would like to ask you if it is possible to double 'S''s aid. I think it is really a question of elementary needs because the family doesn't have any Government help. His wife used to work in a home for deaf people but the Municipality stopped paying salaries so she is doing it now on a voluntary basis.

Since our 2010 visit we had been working with Pastor Oded and Sandy Soshani in Jerusalem. Sandy runs Be'ad Chaim, the Pro-Life organisation and Oded pastors the King of Kings Hebrew speaking Congregation. The Trust responded positively to this request for help for Galila and her daughter:

> Galila is a Jewish Ethiopian single mother with a two-year-old daughter saved through the ministry of Be'ad Chaim. She has worked in factory jobs for several years but since her daughter began day care she suffers frequent illnesses and Galila loses her job because she has to look after her. Galila wants to work and is now cleaning houses but is not earning enough to pay her rent. Please consider helping her immediately. Help for a year would make a tremendous difference. Honestly, the needs in the Ethiopian community are very serious, particularly for a single mother without a family, like Galila.

In the latter half of 2011 the Lord reduced the Trust's funding and in response to prayer He told us that He wanted us to reassess and refine some of our current gifting arrangements before He would increase His provision again. He made it clear that He did not want us to continue with some long-standing support arrangements. He wanted them to cease and there were others that he wanted reduced. He said that there were some people who were looking to Mount Moriah rather than looking to Him. The Trust's support was getting in His way, preventing Him from working in their lives. This was the last thing we ever wanted to happen, and we needed to address it.

Although we found having to discuss cutbacks difficult, only one conversation turned very negative and difficult, but we held our line and carried out the Lord's instructions. Having spoken to everyone, we were most uplifted by the understanding shown by the pastors who thanked and praised the Lord for the generous gifts that they had received in the past. They promised to step up their prayers for the Lord's financial provision.

Ultra-Orthodox activity had increased in Ashdod with believers being followed to their homes and about town. Neighbours were then encouraged to make trouble for them. Around one thousand demonstrated each Sunday outside the Fellowship building.

We had been supporting Pastor Dima and Elmira Brodkin's drug rehabilitation, soup kitchen and church in Beersheva from our very early days. Now in 2011, they were going from strength to strength. There were eight men going through the drug rehabilitation programme and forty-four people attended the soup kitchen on the day of our visit. Food was also parcelled up and taken to those who were ill and unable to attend. They had started an outreach giving out clothes free of charge and so many were glad to find warm clothes for the approaching winter.

Grace House Church was now located in a new building rented from the Municipality. It had been refurbished and fitted out and between fifty and one hundred people were attending the services each week.

Bethlehem was looking a much brighter place and had more life about it in 2011 than in the past. More tourists were staying overnight but it still had the air of an open prison. The security wall and the checkpoint were dominant and most Bethlehemers could not go into Jerusalem. Unemployment was half what it was at its worst but still around 33%. Immanuel Evangelical Church was investing in ministries for the children and the youth to provide them with out-of-school activities part-funded by the Trust. Despite pleas for people to stay and be a light in the darkness, families were still leaving to go abroad in order to provide a better future for their children.

We paid our first visit to Pastor Ariel and Keren Revach in Ramla. We were providing ten food parcels each month for this small Fellowship and wanted to visit some of the families. We visited Bella and her daughter Ella (nine) who is autistic. Bella had to provide 24/7 care as there were no special schools in Ramla that could cope with Ella's needs. Her older daughter Orli was serving in the IDF. We visited Ludmilla, a grandmother who was bringing up her daughter's twin thirteen-year-old sons. The boys had been subjected to cruel physical abuse by their mother and her boyfriend. Eventually it had been agreed that it would be better if the children were brought up by their grandmother. It was a desperate struggle for Ludmilla to provide for all their needs in her tiny apartment.

In Nazareth Pastor Nizar Touma's Church of the Nazarene had attracted a good number of ex-Greek Orthodox and Catholic believers who, in their own words, had 'found Jesus' in the church, prompting accusations from Greek Orthodox and Catholic priests that Nizar *'had stolen their sheep!'*

Once we had returned home, we were delighted and encouraged to find that the Lord honoured us for carrying out His restructuring instructions whilst we had been in Israel. We saw an almost immediate increase in His provision from both the UK and Australia. What a wonderful God we serve!

2012

During our Autumn visit, Tony and I were invited to deliver the message at Cana Baptist Church's Sunday evening service. It was based on the spiritual blessings we have in Christ and was very well received. The church was full and Pastor Hani was praying that the new, larger upper meeting room would be completed before Christmas to cater for the growing numbers.

The Lord had been at work in the church – He had intervened to get the church the licence and insurance for the summer children's camp in one morning, a process that normally takes one month. God had given Pastor Hani & Shifa Billan His message to put their strength into developing the youth as they are the future. As part of this, the church was sponsoring music lessons for a group of children to develop them into the next generation music worship team.

The Ethiopian community in Israel at this time, and especially the Messianic believers were facing a number of difficult challenges. Whilst many of the older generation were finding it difficult to learn Hebrew and integrate into Israeli society, their children were growing up as young Israelis speaking Hebrew at school and with their friends.

This cultural gap extended to Pastor Zechariah Arni's Retzon Ha'El congregation. Until recently the whole service had been conducted in Amharic (the Ethiopian language) for the benefit of the older members but this was starting to change. Hebrew not Amharic was the language of choice for the children. Preserving their Ethiopian cultural identity was important, but unless a way forward could be found that embraced Hebrew, the churches would lose their children altogether, or at best, to other Hebrew speaking congregations. This was already happening in Jerusalem within Pastor Tal's congregation.

The danger was that the gap between parents and children would only get wider as the children got older. The poor educational background of many parents coupled with their lack of Hebrew meant that many were unable to help their children with homework – another way in which these children felt different/disadvantaged from other children in their school.

The problem did not lie only with the parents. The children themselves were suffering from an identity crisis as they did not feel that they were totally accepted as Israelis (because of the colour of their skin) and yet they did not feel Ethiopian either!

The children needed to be comfortable inviting their friends to accompany them to church – which meant that at least their part of praise, worship and teaching needed to be conducted in Hebrew. The Ethiopian pastors understood this, but it would take time to adjust and to plan a strategy that would accommodate the elderly Amharic speakers whilst transitioning the main part of their services to Hebrew. They would have to learn and introduce Hebrew Messianic worship songs, along with preaching and prayer in Hebrew. One thing was certain, the future of the Ethiopian Messianic Congregations depended on the successful transition to Hebrew that would retain and expand the participation of the children and youth.

Whilst visiting Anis and Nawal they took us to meet Aida who had diabetes. She was in considerable pain having been tipped out of her wheelchair when a wheel came off on an uneven pavement in her town. She needed to go to the clinic to get her injuries checked but could not afford the cost of the ambulance to take her there. We gave her the funds to get herself checked over and she went soon after we left.

We also met Nijmi a grandmother who had undertaken the upbringing of one of her son's four children following the break-up of his marriage. She had rung Anis and Nawal to say that she had no food in the house and that she had had to send the children to school without having any breakfast and with nothing for their lunch. We learned that the family had been relying for some time on other people to give them food. It was also the birthday of Naser, one of the boys.

Anis and Nawal quickly went out and bought food so that the family had a nourishing meal when the children got back home from school. They also bought a cake to celebrate Naser's birthday after the service at the House of Light that evening. The Trust committed to supply a financial contribution to provide regular food for Nijmi and the children including chicken, vegetables and fruit. Anis and Nawal were very careful to ensure that the support was used properly – they distributed food parcels and used shopping coupons at specific stores that allowed the coupons only to be used for certain items.

In November we paid our first visit to Christian Arab Pastor Najeeb Atteih and his wife Elizabeth. As well as pastoring congregations in Haifa, Nazareth and Jaffa they ran the Immanuel Christian Book Shop in Haifa. They told us that Christian Arabs in Israel feel forgotten as many people outside Israel think that there are just Jews and Muslims.

Many in their Haifa congregation had difficult backgrounds, broken families etc but despite this they were growing in faith and standing in the Lord. There was much need in the congregation at that time and the congregation was supporting thirteen families with food each month. We provided a gift to help those in need.

The Church of the Nazarene in Nazareth was growing and Pastor Nizar Touma continued to be accused of *"stealing sheep"* from the Greek Orthodox and Catholic flocks. Nazareth at that time was full of religious spirits and the spirits of rejection and denial, just as in Jesus' time.

There was good news of David & Kamilia. David was able to work more and they were taking the opportunity to move to a village further North to be with other family members. David had already obtained a job in the village. The Lord had restored the family, lifting them out of their difficult time and providing them with a positive future.

Pastor Nihad Salman asked us if we could extend our support to help a lady in the Immanuel Evangelical Church in Bethlehem. He told us about the lady whose father and husband had died within a short time of each other leaving her alone and with absolutely no income whatsoever. Her only family was the Church. She had a 3½ year old daughter and cared for her mentally retarded younger brother so would find it difficult to work. The Trust readily agreed to Pastor Nihad's request to provide regular support for her and it was the start of a long and fruitful relationship with the lady and her daughter.

We visited Pastor Yoyakim and Debbie Figueras in Arad, and attended Hasdey Yeshua Fellowship's meeting in the Park on a pleasant Shabbat afternoon. They still did not have an indoor meeting place but were hoping to sign a lease on a building soon.

This year the congregation was helping a group of seventy Christian refugees from the Nuba mountains in North Sudan. Israel would not allow them to work and wanted to repatriate them to North Sudan. The refugees did not want to go back as they feared for their lives if they did. Persecution by Muslims was the reason that they had left in the first place. They wanted to go to South Sudan but the South's government would not accept them as they were from the North. They were in limbo! We were pleased to provide a gift to buy food coupons for them.

Shortly before our visit to Israel, the Lord had reminded us that our ministry is to help believers and He also spoke to us about Orphanages/ Children's homes, something He had put on our hearts for some time.

Pastor Nihad Salman recommended the Home of New Life (HONL) in Ramallah to us and took us to meet Pastor Munir Kakish and his wife Sharon who run the home with their son Michael and his wife Jackie.

Pastor Nihad did not have a permit to drive out of the West Bank at the time so we had to go the long way around rather than through Jerusalem. The journey was an adventure in itself, the route took us a long way through beautiful scenery as we skirted Jerusalem to get to Ramallah. Just to make things more challenging a nail punctured one of the car's tyres and we had to find somewhere to get it fixed. But it was all worth it!

Pastor Munir himself was raised in a home from the age of ten, accepted Christ as his Saviour there and soon afterwards heard the call into ministry. His heart for the children and his empathy for their situation was clear to see.

At the time, HONL was caring for ten boys aged from seven to seventeen, from poor and/or dysfunctional families and they all felt that it was their home. Six of the boys were resident in the home and four came for meals and extra tuition after school before going home. Tutors came to the home every day to help the children with their school work. The boys were supervised by a live-in "House Father" who himself grew up in the home and had now returned to work there. Every day they had Bible study.

The Home teaches the children about love, about Jesus and about respect, it gives them an education and a future. In 2012 fifteen ex-HONL children were studying in college, some at Bible College. It was encouraging to hear that so many children have gone into ministry and leadership within Christ's church or have obtained good jobs and secure futures.

We were blessed to spend a few hours being shown around the home and church complex, meeting the staff and sharing a meal with the children. After the meal they showed us their homework and we met the tutor. Just before we left, there was great excitement when a farmer brought in a live sheep to show the children – it was a gift to the Home to provide them with a supply of meat.

We were so pleased that the Lord had led us to the Home and we pledged to provide regular support for the children through their sponsorship scheme. It would prove to be the start of a very special and fruitful relationship with Pastor Munir & Sharon and the children in the Home.

Having completed our visits in the north, we transferred down to our base in Jerusalem to visits pastors in the centre and south of the country.

Rockets and mortars were being fired into southern Israel from Gaza on an almost daily basis. During the year there were 2,221 rockets and 196 mortars fired from Gaza. Although very few were killed (six) and injured (sixty-nine), having to continuously run to bomb shelters day and night was having a very traumatic impact on the population, especially the children. At the time that we visited Israel Pochtar in Ashdod seventy of his congregation, mainly families with children had gone north to stay at Beit Yedidia, a congregation in Haifa, to get respite away from the barrage of missiles.

Pastor Israel took us on a tour of the town to see some of the damage done by rockets that got past the Iron Dome defence system. It was a miracle that so few missiles had done substantial damage or killed or injured people. There was no doubt in our minds that God was protecting His people.

The families and particularly the children in Ashdod, as in every town under fire in the South, were very stressed but in general the trouble had strengthened the congregation's faith. The food parcels that the Trust was sponsoring on a regular basis were more necessary than ever and Pastor Israel knew that the number of families receiving them would need to be increased for a period. We were pleased to be able to provide additional funds to help him buy the extra provisions that were needed.

In all the years we have visited Israel, we have never felt in danger, we have always trusted in the Lord to keep us safe on our travels around the country. Just as we were leaving Ashdod to return to Jerusalem the air-raid sirens went off and we had to stop the car, get out and lie on the ground against a wall. We heard the booms as the Iron

Dome anti-missile system intercepted and shot down three incoming missiles. When we looked up we could clearly see the missile trails and three puffs of white smoke where they had hit their targets. We praised the Lord for His protection over Israel! When the "all clear" sounded we were able to get back in our car and continue our journey. Just another day in the south of Israel!

We were delighted to visit the Shabbat service at the Grace House Russian Messianic Congregation in Beersheva for the first time in their new building, albeit a week later than originally planned as the meeting had to be cancelled due to the intensive rocket attacks from Gaza. The Church was no longer meeting in the rear courtyard of their house. They had a new church building which was in a different part of town and a different catchment area. It was good to see the Church almost full for the service as the congregation was growing.

What wonderful work Pastor Dima and Elmira Brodkin were doing. From small acorns great oak trees grow! Apart from the church they were running the drug and alchohol rehabilitation centre, the Soup Kitchen three days a week and a Bible College programme attended by twenty people.

When we visited Pastor Ariel Revach in Ramla he took us to meet and pray with some of the families that receive food parcels funded by the Trust each month. There were twenty five families in Ariel's congregation and half were single mums. We met Galia whose husband died in his forties and her young son Adam. We prayed for her health as she had a swelling in her neck. We also met Olissia and her children Mark and Maria. Olissia's husband was an artist who went into drugs and had simply disappeared. It was assumed that he had died. We prayed for the family and for resources to have her dental problems fixed.

We delivered the message that the Lord had given us, to Pastor Tal Shiferaw's congregation at the Shabbat service in Jerusalem. Gashau interpreted for us and there was a visiting Ethiopian Gospel singer named Keffa in attendance. We met a number of the families that the Trust was helping, mainly through food parcels and the baby food and diaper programme. It was a joy to meet families and individuals that the Trust had prayed for and supported in the past and who now are doing well. The Lord has turned around Shelamit's life – a few years previously she had been depressed and suicidal but now she was happily married and had a one-year-old son. How wonderful it was to see! We prayed for the Lord to give Pastor Tal wisdom and patience in his dealings with his church landlord with whom he had a difficult relationship. Misdemeanours such as leaving a light on resulted in fines. It was an unhappy time for Tal who desperately wanted a place the congregation could call their own and use throughout the week.

Our last visit was to Pastor Howard and Randi Bass and the Nachalat Yeshua Congregation in Beer Sheva where we met the families that the Trust prays for and supports. We met Maria but not Dimitri who was getting older and frailer. They were a delightful Russian couple whom we had helped for many years. When they knew that we were visiting the church they always brought us a bag of fruit and a huge jar of honey. We prayed for Dimitri's health and particularly his bad knee which was preventing him from attending the congregation.

2013

During the school summer holidays in Israel Summer Camps are big events for children throughout the Holy Land. However, children from impoverished homes often missed out because their parents could not afford the fees. When the children went back to school and talked to their classmates, those who had missed out felt terribly disadvantaged.

So we were delighted that we were once again able to sponsor twenty children in Pastor Tal's Ethiopian Congregation in Jerusalem to attend Christian Bible Camps. We were also able to sponsor children from other congregations to go to Bible Camp and provide funds for underprivileged children to go on outings to the zoo or a swimming pool etc. What a great opportunity it was to bring joy into the lives of these impoverished children!

The summer is always a busy time for pastors and congregations in the Land. Not only are they arranging activities for the children but also conferences for the whole church family to attend, often meeting up with other congregations to enjoy fellowship together. The idea being to take everyone away together for a short time for fellowship, Bible study, rest and recuperation. These conferences are the only break from everyday routine that many families are able to enjoy.

We prayed for the pastors, elders and ministry leaders who put so much time and effort into arranging and running these activities. We prayed for the Lord's provision for the physical and financial resources and that He would anoint these activities with His Holy Spirit.

Statistics issued at the end of 2012 showed that 62% of Israeli children did not have a full set of workbooks needed for their year of study. These workbooks are very expensive and many families have several children to provide for. When families are struggling to provide the basics of life it is inevitable that children miss out on having these books.

The Lord showed us that the Trust should help as many children as possible to go to school with all the workbooks that they need. It would be an investment in their future which in the long term would offer them the chance to get better jobs and help them to rise out of poverty.

Pastor Munir and Sharon Kakish have always sent us regular updates on the boys in the Home of New Life that the Trust sponsors. For one of their updates they had interviewed the eight boys who were "living in" and had asked them: How is God important to you? Is Jesus your friend and Saviour?

Here are some of the delightful answers that the boys gave:

- *He helps me all the time. He loves me and I love Him. I am always blessed by Him.*
- *I love Jesus, He heals me when I am sick.*
- *He helps me in everything and is always there for me.*
- *He lives in my heart. He created me. He loves me and I love Him.*
- *He helps me. He created us.*

- *He cares about me. He brought me to the Home of New Life. He loves me.*
- *I am learning about God from attending AWANA and kids club.*
- *He helps me not to fall. He loves me and helps sick people.*

During our annual visit in October/November we expected to extend the work to new congregations and families. Shortly after our arrival, we attended the annual meeting of the Messianic Fellowships and Arab Congregations in the North of Israel, in the Lavi Forest outside Tiberias. It was a great opportunity to meet so many pastors in one place. We knew a lot of them already and it was an opportunity to be introduced to those we had not met before. We had been hoping that we would be able to meet Pastor Yossi Ovadia with whom we had corresponded but not met face-to-face. A man was sent over to us to translate for us and, of course, it was Yossi! Thank you Lord.

The main address was given by Pastor Nizar Touma of the Church of the Nazarene in Nazareth. His theme was: *ECHAD "One new man" in Christ – unity and reconciliation*. He emphasised that when there is unity God will respond. Believers in Jesus Christ should stop seeing one another as Jews or Arabs but rather as brothers and sisters in Christ. They should build bridges of love between each other, visit one another's congregations and invite Jewish/Arab pastors to come and speak at each other's churches. This would build strength and unity in the Body and God would respond positively. It was a powerful message and we prayed that the message would be acted upon and that it would produce abundant fruit.

A few days later we visited the Lebanese Church in Nahariyya to attend their service. There we met some Jewish members of the Morning Star Fellowship in Tiberias who had heard Pastor Nizar's message, taken it to heart and acted upon it.

Pastor Hani and Shifa Billan invited us to attend the baptism in the River Jordan at Yardenit of three young people from their extended family. Those baptised were their daughter Marlene, Ibrahim and

Ekhlas' daughter Heba, and Adel and Sahar's son Nizar. Ibrahim is Shifa's brother and Sahar is her sister. What a wonderful and very special day it was for the family and everyone in the church who came along to support. It was such a privilege to be able to share in this special occasion.

Pastor Claude Ezagouri reported that the spiritual climate in Tiberias was improving. Believers had a good reputation in the city and people were more open to them. However, life continued to be difficult for many in the congregation for without charity many would not survive in Israel.

Lena, one of the ladies that the Trust helped, told Claude's wife Michelle at the Shabbat service that her son was not working and they had no food in the house. It was God's gracious timing that we had with us a gift for her from her prayer partner family in England. We prayed that the government would stop procrastinating and give her citizenship as without it she had no medical cover if she fell ill. We prayed for the Lord's divine intervention.

'M' and 'S' the two Druze believers in the congregation were under extreme pressure in their village to renounce their faith. They were suffering much persecution and harassment. 'M' and his wife had no water in their house due to a problem with pipes under the floor. Both 'M' and 'S' were very grateful for the help that they received from the Trust and we prayed that the Lord would give both families strength and perseverance in their time of trouble.

We were delighted to forge a new partnership with Pastor Yossi and Ronit Ovadia and Kehilat Haderech (The Way) in Karmiel, a town between Tiberias and Akko (Acre) in the north of Israel. We visited them at their worship building in the industrial part of town, met the staff and learned about the challenges that the church and the congregation faced in this part of Israel.

Helping children's education and the youth was a subject close to all our hearts and we agreed that the Trust would provide funds to purchase workbooks and text books for children whose families could not afford them. We would also contribute funds to sponsor youth activities including a winter camp. This was the start of another lasting and fruitful relationship.

When we saw Pastor Nizar and Katy Touma at the Church of the Nazarene in Nazareth it was encouraging to hear how families that had been in difficulty were now doing well having been helped in their time of need. Sadly Adel, whom we had been helping since 2008, had died of his cancer.

It was sad to hear that the Christian population of Nazareth had dropped from 70% in the 1970s down to only 30% and that one in five of the town's population was unemployed. Christians were emigrating to escape the antagonism and intimidation from the Muslim majority and to find a better life and a more hopeful future for their children. We prayed for the future and protection of Christian children and young people who were not enjoying life in Nazareth. So many Muslim children were into drugs and alcohol that it made for a very unpleasant environment.

We spent a day with Anis and Nawal Barhoum in Shefar'am visiting families and distributing food, mattresses, blankets and other essentials to needy families. Anis and Nawal have a great heart to care for the innocent wives and children of Christians that they meet in their prison ministry.

We travelled as far as Fassuta a Christian village close to the Lebanese border to take mattresses for the three children of a prisoner. We took blankets and other bedding materials to single mum Amira. With winter approaching, these would help her and her six sons cope with the cold nights. Her apartment was very bare, was not in very good repair and only had a wood burning stove for heating.

Seventeen families were receiving support of one kind or another through the Trust and once again we were encouraged to hear that so many families had recovered from their hard times and were better able to provide for themselves. The fruits of standing alongside people in their time of need were very evident wherever we went.

Pastor Hani and Shifa Billan at Cana Baptist Church told us about the important discipleship and guidance they are providing to Christian children and youths in Cana. One hundred and fifteen children had attended the six day CBC Summer Bible Camp. Thirty-five children were from CBC families and eighty from Catholic and Orthodox families. Since the Orthodox Church in Cana had closed its youth club and summer Camp, CBC had been left to fill this important role – a challenge that they were delighted to take up. The weekly CBC youth meeting was also attracting youths from Orthodox and Catholic churches. We were so pleased that the Trust had been able to contribute funds to support the camp and that it had been such a positive influence on so many children.

We visited Pastor Zechariah Arni in Haifa whom we had been supporting since 2007 to hear how his Ethiopian Messianic congregation in Haifa was progressing. As well as pastoring the church, Zechariah is the manager of the municipal social centre in his local area working with children and the youth. He shared with us pictures of the children from the Kehilat enjoying a day out at a theme park during their summer holidays which the Trust had funded. It was a great treat for the children and it gave them something special to share with their classmates when they went back to school.

We prayed for Zechariah's wife, Alemaz who was pregnant expecting their fourth child to be born around 5th January 2014. We prayed for her health as she suffers from Type 1 diabetes and has to take insulin four times a day. This was the first time that we had become aware of her condition and the cost of her daily treatment and other special dietary needs which are not covered by their health insurance. We felt touched by the Lord that the Trust should cover these costs in future.

For a number of years the Trust had sponsored food parcels for the many needy families in the Kehilat so this year we went out with Zechariah to make deliveries to families in their homes. The apartments were very basic, and often in desperate need of repair.

We met Ethiopian families where the parents were struggling to learn to speak, read and write Hebrew. This was not uncommon within the Ethiopian community. At the extreme, there were families where the parents could not communicate with their children who were growing up as young Israelis wanting and expecting to speak Hebrew at all times.

Pastor Nizar Touma took us to visit Yousef Matta at his home in the Christian village of Eilabun near Tiberias. Yousef was a very skilled wood carver and we wanted to see if he could help us to inscribe some olive wood hearts we had bought. We wanted to give each of the ladies that I would be talking to a heart inscribed with her name. He showed us many of his wonderful wood carvings and said that it would be no problem to do the inscriptions.

Yousef was very proud of the sycamore-fig tree that was in his garden, he told us that it was the last known sycamore-fig tree in the north of Israel. We had never seen this unusual tree before and were able to taste the small sweet figs that grow in clusters out of the trunk and branches. Of course, it reminded us of Jesus' encounter with Zacchaeus and very much brought it to life. It would have been a relatively easy tree to climb.

Zacchaeus climbed a sycamore-fig tree to see Jesus Luke 19:2-6

We were also able to visit Yousef's daughter Kamilia whom the Trust had helped when she lived in Nazareth. She had moved to Eilabun and it was good to see her and to hear that the family were doing well having got through the difficult time following her husband David's accident.

The Hasdey Yeshua Congregation in Arad switched their Shabbat meeting from the open air in the forest to someone's house as rain was forecast. This was something that happened regularly during the winter as the congregation continued to search for a permanent meeting place. Recent hopes had been dashed once the property owner learned that they were a Messianic congregation – so they continued to search. The Trust's prayer partners spent much time asking that the Lord would lead the congregation to the right place.

The seventy North Sudanese that the congregation had been assisting in 2012 had been dispersed across Israel but they were now helping a South Sudanese family with three children with food coupons.

We travelled to Ashdod to meet Pastor Israel Pochtar and Pastor Ariel Revach who updated us on the needs of his very poor congregation. The Trust was helping ten families every month with 150 Shekel supermarket cards that enabled them to buy groceries (but not alcohol or cigarettes). We prayed for Ariel's health as he was in a lot of pain from a stomach ulcer and had lost a lot of weight as a result of the eating difficulties this was causing.

Pastor Israel invited us to speak to a meeting of Russian Jewish believers and non-believers to explain to them why a UK based Christian Charity provided spiritual and financial support to the people of Israel. It was a great opportunity to share what the Bible says about Israel and the Jews. We explained about the spiritual blessings that we Gentile believers have received from the Jews and then we explained from the scriptures God's plans for Israel and the Jewish people.

For if the Gentiles have shared in the Jews spiritual blessings, they owe it to the Jews to share with them their material blessings. Romans 15:27

The next day, we were picked up outside the Mamilla Mall at the Jaffa Gate in Jerusalem and taken through the checkpoint and on to Ramallah to spend the day at the Home of New Life. This year we met Michael and Jackie Kakish who now run the home on a day to day basis and spent a wonderful afternoon with the staff and children. As soon as the children got home from school we had lunch with them. After lunch and a short play time the tutors arrived and the children settled down to their homework. There were six boys who were "living in" and another eight who came to the home for meals and tuition before going home at night. The Trust was providing sponsorship for each of the fourteen boys so it was good to meet them all and see first-hand how they were doing.

145

This year the Trust made a new commitment to support Pastor Dov Bikas' Aviv Ministry amongst drug addicts and prostitutes in Tel Aviv. We visited Dov at the Aviv Centre located next to the old bus station in the south of Tel Aviv. It was a run down area around the derelict and dilapidated concrete base of the old bus station. Drug addicts were living in the open in ramshackle temporary shelters and the surrounding area was a centre for prostitution.

The Aviv Centre, staffed by volunteer groups from various churches, provides daily meals, clothes, blankets, a toilet and a place for the homeless to shower and change their clothes. We accompanied Dov on his "Coca Cola ministry" to visit the drug and alcohol addicted men and women living on the street. Offering a cup of Coca Cola gave Dov an opening to talk to them and tell them about the facilities at the Aviv Centre. Those who visit the centre are told about the Gospel and the love of Jesus and are counselled to save their lives by attending a Drug Rehab centre. It was a good balance between practical love and the Gospel.

It was a real eye opener to see so many people living like this and the terrible physical shape they are in. We saw things that shocked us; people walking around with needles hanging out of their bodies, people being injected in their necks as they searched for veins that had not been damaged. There were needles everywhere on the ground, it was a very dangerous place to walk. Heroin and cocaine were bad enough, but the synthetic drugs that had replaced them do irreparable damage to the body and brain. Whilst walking the streets we felt very strongly that if Jesus had been back on the earth that day, this is where He would have been ministering.

Praise the Lord, many have been saved through the Aviv Ministry and remarkably a significant number of those attending the Russian speaking course at Netanya Bible College that year were ex-addicts.

Dov describes the Aviv Centre as **"the last stop before the cemetery"** for many people. But for those who respond it is the start of a journey:

"From **Coca Cola** to **Aviv Centre** to **Rehab** to **Church** and finally to **Heaven**." **Hallelujah !!!**

On Sunday we were picked up at the Bethlehem checkpoint to attend the morning service at Immanuel Evangelical Church. It was good to meet the congregation and to enjoy the service with them. Afterwards we had lunch and spent time with Pastor Nihad and Salwa Salman.

The economic situation in Bethlehem was still bad with 38% unemployed (within the church about 20%). We were asked to pray especially for young graduates leaving college with degrees who cannot find work. If they could not find work after two to three years they would leave the country. This situation was having a negative effect on children studying at school and they were starting to question if all the hard work was worth it.

The IEC ministry focus was very much on the young with three full time ministries for children, teenagers/youth and young adults. The outstanding news was the amazing success of the Church's Mr OK Theatre. The show gave a message of forgiveness and acceptance: God forgave us by sending Jesus – so we should forgive others. The Palestinian Authority Ministry of Education had heard about the show and sent an official to see a performance. As a result they invited Mr OK to visit ALL schools in the West Bank – they are all Muslim schools! By the end of the year the show would have been seen by 25,000 children aged seven to fourteen. We prayed that the small seeds sown in the children's hearts would lead them to find their Saviour.

The House of Grace Ministry in Beer Sheva run by Pastor Dima & Elmira Brodkin was growing and expanding into new areas. The soup kitchen operating three times a week was feeding over 150 each week including twenty-two holocaust survivors. Clothes distribution was taking place weekly at the church and families were receiving Bibles along with their clothes. Eleven people would soon graduate and get their diplomas at the end of their Bible College studies. Since the Drug Rehabilitation Centre had started four hundred men had passed through and had their lives touched by the Lord. They were planning new projects including visiting Jews in the former Soviet Union to encourage them to make Aliyah then offering them assistance and guidance to settle in Israel. Dima and Elmira knew from personal experience that the transition to a new and different land was very difficult and that people needed help to transition successfully.

The Ethiopian Messianic Kehilat Beit El congregation in Jerusalem was growing spiritually and becoming more fruitful. However, 35 children and their families had left the church much to Pastor Tal Shiferaw's distress. The families had moved to a Hebrew speaking congregation because the children preferred it, despite some of the adults understanding very little of the service. The problem that we had forseen in 2012 had started to happen. The children were growing up as young Israelis doing everything in Hebrew but Tal's Shabbat service was still being conducted in Amharic because many of the older members could not speak or read Hebrew. Although the Sunday school was being conducted in Hebrew it was not enough to retain the children. It was a very difficult problem for Pastor Tal to solve and we prayed for the Lord to give him wisdom.

The Trust's financial support and food parcel programme was providing essential relief to many members of the congregation who were elderly, poor and not in good health.

The Messianic Ethiopian community was facing regular and open attacks. A Rabbi in the Knesset had said that "Ethiopians are not really Jewish and you should not marry them." An Israeli Ethiopian radio programme was constantly speaking against the believers and arguing that they should all be deported back to Ethiopia. The Messianic Ethiopians in Israel needed the Lord to give them strength of character, determination and the will to resist and withstand such abuse.

Another new partnership forged this year was the commitment to support the Christian House of Hope in Bethlehem which cares for the blind and children with special needs. On the day we visited, there were ten boys and six girls resident in the home and in addition to the chidren, there are five older men and five blind adults living in the Home.

It was amazing to see the skill and dexterity of two blind men making brushes and brooms in the workshop. The United Nations bought most of the brooms and others were sold locally. This gave the men an occupation, self esteem and earned them pocket money. Four mentally handicapped men were making olive wood souvenirs under supervision for sale in the shop. Again the work helps the men's self esteem and provides them with pocket money.

Most of the residents were from Muslim backgrounds but everyone attends "Devotions" twice a day where they sing worship songs, hear and discuss the Gospel and pray together. One teenager we met during our tour of the Home insisted that we pray for him. Whilst visiting his parents the previous weekend he had damaged his hand and had to go to hospital and he insisted that we pray with him for his healing. It was very touching!

In summary, during this visit the Lord had *"enlarged the place of our tent"* by extending partnerships to Pastor Yossi Ovadia at Kehilat Haderech in Karmiel, Pastor Dov Bikas and the Aviv Ministry in Tel Aviv and the House of Hope in Bethlehem.

The emphasis was three fold:

1. helping children to get a good education that would give them hope for the future;
2. helping the youth and young adults to grow in the Lord and join in Jewish-Arab reconciliation;
3. reaching out to the blind, the disabled, the drug addicts and the desperate – those on the fringes of society.

We felt the presence of the Lord was very much with us as we made our visits. We lifted our eyes to Jesus the Great Shepherd whose heart is for the poor and needy. We praised and thanked the Lord for each one of the Trust's supporters for none of this would have been possible without the wonderful support that they provide. We could reassure everyone that their prayers and financial support

GO TO THE LAND OF MORIAH

were making a difference in the lives of so many people.

As Claude Ezagouri said: **"without charity many could not survive here in Israel."**

> *May the God of hope fill you with all joy and peace as you trust in him, so that you may overflow with hope by the power of the Holy Spirit.* Romans 15:13

150

Chapter 18

Mount Moriah Trust 2014 – 2017

2014

2014 started on a sad note as in January our Patron Ken Burnett, the founder of Prayer For Israel, was called home to be with the Lord. He had been a wonderful advisor and encourager and a major influence in getting the Mount Moriah Trust established. He would be greatly missed by everyone who knew him.

When our financial year ended on 31st May we summarised the support that was being provided. The trust was working with sixteen Messianic Pastors and nine Arab Pastors to provide spiritual and financial support and encouragement to believers in Israel, Gaza and the West Bank.

The practical support included:

- Help to buy food and other essentials for needy families;
- Approximately one hundred food parcels every month for the neediest families including widows, the elderly and single mums;
- Medicines including the insulin treatment and special diet for the wife of a pastor;
- Children's school workbooks and text books;
- Sponsorship for children from poor homes to attend Christian Bible camps;
- Sponsorship for youths to attend Christian youth camps and

conferences especially those that brought Jewish and Arab youths together in reconciliation;
- Contributions towards pastors' salaries to enable them to support their families and perform effectively as pastors;
- Sponsorship of Christian soup kitchens and drug rehabilitation centres;
- Sponsorship for children from poor and dysfunctional families to attend the Christian "Home of New Life" in Ramallah;
- Sponsorship of the Christian "House of Hope" for the blind and mentally handicapped children in Bethlehem.

According to government statistics one third of the population of Israel was living on or below the poverty line and the situation had worsened as a result of the war with Hamas in Gaza. Increasing numbers were going days without food and their refrigerators were empty. However, with the help of our supporters the Trust was making a difference in the lives of so many people. That summer we were blessed to be able to provide sponsorship for children to attend summer camps. The importance of these camps is demonstrated by the reports that we received from the pastors:

Pastor Munir and Sharon Kakish at The Home of New Life in Ramallah wrote:

We want to thank you for your prayers and support for our summer camp.

Praise God for the opportunity to teach seventy-five children about Jesus and the Eternal Life He offers all; the Bible verses the children memorized to hide God's word in their hearts including John 11:26 *"Whoever lives by believing in Me will never die"*; the wonderful staff willingly pouring God's love into the children's lives; the wonderful time that everyone had.

This year's theme was Jesus is my Hero and all the children

wore their "Super Hero" shirts whilst learning Bible stories and verses and doing craft. The children learnt so much of Jesus and of His salvation. They loved our camp.

This is what your prayers and funds do in the Holy Land. Thank you for partnering with us.

Pastor Yossi Ovadia in Karmiel wrote about the Kehilat Haderech Youth Camp

We thank you for standing with us in prayer and funding for our youth camp. The camp was very blessed and rich with wonderful experiences. We thank the Lord for the blessed time we had together with our youth.

Pastor Zechariah Arni, Kehilat Retzon Ha'El in Haifa wrote

The children's camp was very successful and the children were very happy. For all of them it was a great privilege. Without this camp they would finish the summer vacation and go back to school without any experience.

Thank you for your support, as without your support those children could not receive this kind of activity. Thank you for all the blessings and the love that you show us.

Pastor Tal Shiferaw, Kehilat Beit El in Jerusalem wrote:

Dear my family thank you so much for your help. This year we have been able to extend our children's program. In addition to the ten children who attended camp in Jerusalem we have been able to send, for the first time, five children over fourteen years old to camp in Tiberias.

Pastor Hani & Shifa Billan at Cana Baptist Church wrote:

Dear Partners. We are very thankful for your prayers and support for the camp. It was a blessed camp – there were one hundred and forty children aged five to fourteen who participated.

2015

Our annual visit to the Pastors was quite hectic. We had forty-three meetings, some all day, and made four new commitments. We met with all our partner pastors except one and attended a pastors' breakfast meeting in Jerusalem where we met a number of pastors that we had not met before.

What a difference a year had made! In 2014 Pastor Tal Shiferaw, Kehilat Beit El in Jerusalem had been very down, but the Lord had fully restored him and had provided him with a new meeting place. What an answer to prayer! Before signing a contract for the building, Tal had sought out and found a partner to share in the rent. This was a very wise move because rents in Jerusalem are exorbitant and it would be very hard for the congregation to manage the cost on its own.

God led us to the Eritrean refugee community in Southern Tel Aviv and to Pastor Sibhat Petros and the Gospel For All The Nation Church in Tel Aviv. This thriving church had a congregation of over two hundred and fifty, most of whom had been saved since arriving in Israel. Israel was the reluctant host to around 35,000 Eritrean refugees whose status is "temporary non-deportation". They had no social rights or access to any social, welfare or health services and they were not officially allowed to work, but of course, they had to work in order to survive. They worked for cash at below the minimum wage in construction, hotels, restaurants etc. When new babies were registered the authorities only registered the mother's name and not the fathers to avoid giving the family any rights to residency in Israel. Because of their status they were allowed only a very basic bank account, no cheque book and no credit card. We could not send them cheques as their bank would not accept them, so we arranged to send gifts to them via one of the Ethiopian pastors. It would be a privilege to be able to stand alongside the families in this church.

In keeping with the direction that the Lord had given us to help the youth to strengthen and encourage their walk with the Lord, we started to support the work of Lech L'cha, a ministry equipping young believers for life and ministry. They run various programs including a three-month discipleship programme and a ten day "Netsor" Pre-IDF program. Students have to raise the necessary funds to cover the cost of attendance but despite their best efforts, sometimes they would fall short. The Trust has partnered with Lech L'cha to provide a top-up fund that could be used at their discretion to make up the shortfall in a student's funding. This year two students on the three-month discipleship programme had benefitted from the scheme.

In Haifa Pastor Najeeb Atteih's Christian Soldiers Centre was taking shape. One container was in place and a second was expected soon. The centre would provide a much needed place of rest, refreshment and encouragement for believers serving in the IDF, particularly the 500+ Christian Arabs who had volunteered. The Sunday School had been established after demand from both children and parents for a more permanent programme following the summer camp. Operating from 0800 to 1400 every Sunday it provided Bible study and worship for children aged three to eleven. Attendance was expected to grow to 40 children by the end of the year. We were so pleased that we were able to support both these activities.

Jay Rawlings invited us to attend a pastors' breakfast in Jerusalem at which the Lord put us together with an Arab brother, Pastor Vincent Shammas from the Good God Church in East Jerusalem which had a 50 strong congregation. Vincent was and still is one of very few Arab Pastors who believes in God's plans for Israel and does not subscribe to replacement theology. Because of this, he and his church were isolated and needed financial and spiritual support and encouragement. We felt strongly that the Lord had put us together for a purpose and that we should develop the relationship further and support his ministry.

We discovered through Pastor Israel Pochtar, that while we were going to be in Jerusalem, the Trust's Patron David Hathaway would be holding two meetings in Tel Aviv to evangelize to Holocaust Survivors and their families. We were invited to one of the meetings and were blessed to spend some time with David and have him pray for us and the work. Two thousand people attended the meetings over the two days.

2016

Feedback that we were receiving from the pastors and leaders of organisations that we were working with said that "God was changing lives in His Land through the Mount Moriah Trust." God continued to "enlarge the place of our tent" as new relationships were forged during the year. Mount Moriah trustee Mark Dunman and his wife Margaret visited a number of pastors and congregations in the north of Israel in May which resulted in new relationships in Afula and Nazareth Illit.

We started a new relationship with Pastor Yakov Dolinsky and the Rock of My Salvation Congregation in Nazareth Illit, following Mark and Margaret's visit. The Fellowship had a sixty-five strong congregation including children and they met in a rented warehouse building which was getting run down and too small for the congregation's needs. The congregation was not well off and was not able to support a pastor which meant that Yakov had to work. He had little time to pastor or prepare his sermons and every time he took time off work to attend a conference or other ministry matter he lost money from his salary. It was agreed that the Trust would provide him with a contribution towards his salary that would enable him to support his family and devote more time to the ministry.

Mark also visited Hanna Haustein in Afula and found a similar problem with Pastor Fyodor Blinder who had taken over leadership of the Yizreel Valley Fellowship, founded by Hanna's husband Herman who had passed away in 2014. Fyodor was also leading small groups in Afula and Beit She'an every week. He worked full-time as a night guard which meant that his time for ministry work was limited. We agreed to provide him with a contribution to his salary so that he would be able to work less, maybe a day less per week and be able to give more time for the ministry.

Pastor Dov Bikas wrote to us with news of the Aviv Ministry and the rehab centre in Beersheva:

> Our ministry is doing well, praise the Lord. Our rehab centre in Beersheva works at full capacity: with five "old" and four "new" guys, all at different stages of rehabilitation and of spiritual progress. Alexei is very busy with each of them, and this is not at all easy. Eduard is busy too, preparing our outreach centre in Tel Aviv for the cold winter season. He has written a thank you letter for you:
>
>> Greetings to you, dear brothers and sisters!
>>
>> Our family sincerely thanks God for your caring hearts. Your financial support gives me the opportunity to be more dedicated to serving in Aviv Centre because I do not need to think about money matters and can spend more time with the people who need our help. I come to Aviv Centre (which is 53km from my city) more frequently now to be able to take care of more people. Soon the cold rainy season begins in Israel, and we want to be able to open Aviv Centre at nights, so that the street people could have shelter from winter weather. Meanwhile we have got only one "night shift" a week, and this is obviously not enough. We need additional volunteers and resources for that, of course.
>>
>> We appreciate your prayers and support and thank our Lord Jesus for you from the bottom of our hearts!
>>
>> Respectfully yours,
>> Eduard Bitiev

The Trust started a new relationship during the year with Pastor Ariel Ben-David and his Maayan Eilat Messianic Congregation in Eilat. The congregation was planted in 2008 by the Beit Hallel Congregation in Ashdod and had grown to around fifty adult members and twenty-five children.

Pastor Ariel and his wife Yael have three daughters and came to Israel from Belarus. As he did not receive a salary from the congregation, he worked two jobs – in the local newspaper and in a travel company. He was praying that as the congregation grew, there would come a time when it could provide him with a salary and he would be able to devote himself to full time ministry.

One of the major difficulties for believers in Eilat is that they are so far away from central Israel where most of the Messianic conferences and other activities take place. This was particularly affecting the youth in the congregation who had little contact with other believers of their own age. We agreed with Pastor Ariel that the Trust would provide regular funds to help and encourage the youth in their walk with the Lord by helping them to travel to fellowship with their peers.

One day we received this request from Pastor Claude Ezagouri – The Morning Star Fellowship in Tiberias:

> Dear Tony & Kathy
>
> I hope everything is well with you. 'M''s daughter doesn't have a bed. She has been sleeping with the parents so far but she is a big girl now and 'M' has to sleep on the floor which is painful because of his back. Do you think you could help the family with a bed and a mattress? The cheapest would be around 1400 NIS (roughly 280 Pounds).
>
> Thank you for any help in this matter.
>
> Claude E.
>
> P.S. 'M' is in the hospital on low B12

'M' is a Druze believer who suffers from poor health and a great deal of harassment and persecution from the population of his Druze village. We were delighted to be able to provide the funds so that all the family could sleep in their own beds.

"Israel's child poverty rate is worse than Mexico and Chile" was the news headline following the publication of a UNICEF report. Israel had the highest level of inequality among children in the world's 41 most developed countries according to UNICEF. The rate of child poverty was the highest amongst the countries ranked. As one MK said: "the reality is that children go to school hungry and parents have difficulty finding the money to pay for children's dental care or textbooks."

LATET, an NGO working with the poor had issued its Poverty Report in November which found that 2,624,000 people (31.9%) of the population lived in poverty in 2015. (These reports always referred to the year before the report's issue date so November 2016 reported on the situation in 2015.) Of these 1,626,000 were adults and 998,000 (more than 1 in 3) were children. It also found that 12% of the needy population was forced to beg on the street for food or search for food in the garbage. In addition, 54% of poor people had their water or electricity disconnected during the past year as they were unable to pay their bills.

The Israel Government's Poverty Report, published around the same time, presented a different picture finding 1,709,300 living below the poverty line which included:

- 444,900 families
- 776,500 children
- 180,000 elderly including 45,000 Holocaust Survivors.

The explanation for the discrepancy between the two reports is that while the Government figures were based on income alone, the LATET figures to determine poverty were based on a person's shortages in five categories – each reflecting essential needs to live with dignity: housing, education, health, food security and the ability to meet the cost of living.

The LATET report found that 96% of the elderly could not afford nursing care or help at home, while 52% were unable to afford medicine or medical treatments and 43% suffered from malnutrition because they are unable to afford basic food. Poor health increased the need for medicines and medical treatment that they could not afford – it was a vicious cycle!

Gidi Kroch, CEO of the Israel National Food Bank said: If the status quo stays as it is, poverty and hunger will continue to hit us harder than our enemies from the outside.

So poverty was still a real issue for so many in Israel, Jews and Arabs alike. Those living under Hamas and the Palestinian Authority were in an even more difficult situation than those in Israel. In Israel there were small, but inadequate social support payments, but in the Palestinian Authority areas there were none.

Our pastor colleagues in the Land sent their heartfelt thanks to all the Trust's supporters for their prayers and financial support – it really was making a difference and lives were being changed for the better.

This was the first year since the Trust started that we did not make a personal visit to the pastors in Israel. Tony's mother had died in April and the sale of her house was taking a long time to complete. It would have been difficult to go away before the details were finalised. We were also planning a three-month ministry trip to Malaysia, Singapore and Australia to promote the work starting in December so we decided that it would have been too much to attempt to visit Israel in October/November.

Our absence was mitigated by the fact that Trustee Mark Dunman and his wife Margaret had visited pastors during the year so there had been some personal contact with our partners.

2017

Early in the year we received a message from Ethiopian Messianic Pastor Tal Shiferaw in Jerusalem:

Shalom Dear My Family

I would like to thank you from my heart for your faithfulness to our work here in Jerusalem. Your help has been instrumental in moving our congregation forward in so many ways. Our youth are growing in the Lord each week. The elderly are enjoying worship and comfort in their days and time with us. The stress that would otherwise be attached to some of the things we do is taken away when the gift you give is applied. There are not enough words to thank you my family. As the congregation grows in the Lord, and moves forward in Him, we know that your contribution is a big part of the reason.

We love you, we pray for you and all the time you are on our hearts. I want to tell you this.

Pastor Tal

Ultra-Orthodox persecution and harassment was on the increase with a number of Messianic leaders and congregations under attack including in Ashdod, Beer Sheva, and Dimona. Landlords were being pressured not to rent or renew leases for buildings or apartments to Messianic believers.

This was borne out when around August we received the following message from Pastor Yakov Dolinsky in Nazareth Illit:

Dear brethren and prayer partners,

Shalom! We are in urgent need of your prayer support. Today I received a phone call from the owner of the building where our fellowship holds meetings. He said that because of our activities the Orthodox Jews made a tremendous pressure on him to stop his contract with us which is supposed to end in 2019. We've been renting this place from him for twenty years and never been late with payments even one day. We turned the place from a warehouse into a "palace". We just finished a big renovation of the building and invested in it more than $15,000. A month before the renovation we had a talk with the owner. He promised that he wouldn't sell the building, and that he would extend our contract after the current one ends, that is in 2019. Now the owner wants us to leave within two or three months by our own will quietly.

Besides your prayers, a legal advice will be very much appreciated.

May God bless you!

Yakov Dolinsky

The postscript to this was that Pastor Yakov held out and saw his contract through to 2019. He had to find a new place once the contract expired and the money spent on renovation benefitted the congregation for only a short time. Ironically it was this renovation work that had attracted the attention of the ultra-Orthodox who ran a soup kitchen from a building a few metres down the street. Until that time they had been unaware of the church's existence but the renovation work had made them curious to know who their neighbour was.

We find that God communicates with us in so many different ways. On the flight from London to Tel Aviv at the start of our annual visit to Israel, the inflight magazine spoke to us through a caption under a picture of a boy wheeling a wheelbarrow full of fruits – so full that it could not carry them all: "Small seeds sown reap fruitful rewards"

The Lord was telling us how the seeds the Trust is sowing into the body of Christ in His Land are producing a bounteous harvest. This inspirational vision was borne out by everything that we saw and heard during our time in the Land. We might have thought that our seeds, our gifts, were small, but He was turning them into something much bigger! We were further reminded of the impact of sowing small seeds when we visited Tel Dan the ancient Biblical town of Dan in the north of Israel. A small acorn had taken root and been transformed into a magnificent Tabor Oak tree.

Wherever we went, we saw the effect that the Trust's gifts were having. To the recipient the gift was not just money but also prayers, love, encouragement, hope and the knowledge that they were not alone in their struggle, they knew that they had people standing alongside them, caring about them. This was having a big impact on each individual life.

All that we have accomplished You have done for us. Isaiah 26:12

The work of Jesus is best done by Jesus Himself. He was *"enlarging the place of our tent"* by leading us to support new pastors and congregations and encouraging us to increase support to existing beneficiaries so that even more could be achieved!

We had met Pastor Efraim & Jeannie Goldstein in the UK earlier in the year and had arranged to visit them in Nahariyya in the north of Israel near the border with Lebanon. They introduced us to Lebanese couple Pierre & Maggie Altounian who assisted Efraim and acted as pastor when he was away. Pierre also had an outreach ministry to the many Lebanese who had moved to Israel after the war with Hezbollah in southern Lebanon. We agreed that the Trust would help Pierre and Maggie by providing a contribution to a salary that would enable Pierre to devote more time to ministry.

Michael & Natasha Milevsky in Afula have an outreach ministry that provides humanitarian relief to ex-Ukrainian Jews from Chernobyl, the site of the 1986 nuclear disaster. So many of those who had made Aliyah are now suffering from cancer. Michael and Natasha have a large family and were themselves living on a pittance. The Trust agreed to support them so that they can raise their family whilst conducting their vital ministry among this needy group of people.

Pastor Zechariah Arni was fast developing into a leader of the Ethiopian Messianic body in the Land and through his recommendation we started to support the New Covenant Ethiopian Messianic Congregation in Tel Aviv led by Pastor Gabi Bezuneh.

Our relationship with Eric Benson and the team at Beit Nitzachon (The House of Victory) Rehabilitation Centre in Haifa went way back to 2006. We had always included them in our prayer letters but had not provided funds to Beit Nitzachon since Grisha had left. Our support for Grisha had continued until he became established in his work at the school for the disabled. When we visited Eric at Beit Nitzachon we knew that things were tough financially and we were strongly led by the Lord to restart providing financial help for the running of the centre.

Providing contributions to pastors' salaries was something relatively new for the Trust but when we talked to the pastors who had received this help we were so impressed by the impact that these fairly small contributions had made that we felt compelled by the Lord to increase them in order to multiply the fruit.

The Trust had grown so much since the DVDs "The Heart of God" Parts 1 & 2 were made in 2009 that we again commissioned Jay Rawlings of Israel Vision, to make a new documentary featuring the thirteen new pastors and organisations that we had started to partner with since those original DVDs had been made. We invited each pastor to talk about their congregation, the challenges that they faced and the benefits of the support that they receive. The video would provide an insight into what life was like and, in many ways still is, for pastors and believers in the Holy Land. All three parts of the DVD can be found on the Trust's website: mountmoriah.org.uk

Pastor Zechariah Arni with the help of sponsorship from an American group organised a conference in Haifa for the Ethiopian and Eritrean community from all across Israel. We were privileged to attend the conference and meet the Ethiopian and Eritrean pastors and members of their congregations many of whom we knew. The theme of the conference was Unity in the Body of Christ in the Land. The Ethiopian Messianic body was growing but there was a need for the pastors to work much more closely together. We prayed with them for the Lord's help to bring them together in unity, to co-operate with one another, become stronger and be more effective in their Kingdom work as a result.

Israel continued to have the largest gap between rich and poor of any country in the developed world. We praised the Lord that the disabled had been granted an increased allowance and there were discussions on increasing allowances for the elderly but there were still over 2.5 million living on or below the poverty line including almost one million children. There was still no help available to the poor in Palestinian Authority administered areas. Life for the citizens of Gaza was "beyond humanitarian crisis and on the verge of total systems failure" according to the UN Middle East envoy.

ISIS activity in northern Egypt had made it very unsafe for Pastor Hanna Maher and his family to return to Gaza after a trip to Egypt to complete his training and visit family. However, conditions had improved sufficiently for him and his family to be able to return to provide much needed leadership and encouragement to the diminishing congregation of Gaza Baptist Church (GBC). The Trust has been providing a contribution to Pastor Hanna Maher's salary through Pastor Hanna Massad, the one-time Pastor of GBC who still makes regular visits to Gaza to uplift and encourage them. The residents of Gaza were living in desperate conditions which were deteriorating all the time.

Tony and I certainly had an eventful time. Although he did not tell me at the time, from the day after we arrived in Tiberias, Tony started getting cramps and pains in his legs which progressively got worse. Then, a few days after arriving in Jerusalem and within an hour of meeting a new pastor and promising support, I fell and broke the humerus bone in my arm at the shoulder. Until it happens, you do not realize what you cannot do when you only have one arm! Washing, dressing, applying medication, getting my hair done and preparing ourselves took almost until lunchtime each day. Tony became "Antoine" an apprentice hairdresser and had to learn how to put in heated rollers.

We had to abandon our visit schedule and eventually went home a week early thanks to British Airways who allowed us to change our booking without charge.

Tony did not want to add to the worries that I had with my broken arm so he did not tell me about the problems he was having until after we got home. Only then did I learn that by the end of our stay the pain in both Tony's legs at the end of each day was so intense that he could hardly walk. I did not know but the Lord knew. One day, Pastor Tal Shiferaw came to the apartment to pray for us. Having prayed for me, he then turned to Tony and said "God has told me to pray for your legs" which he then proceeded to do. Tony was amazed that God had told Tal when he, Tony had told no-one and still did not tell me even then!

Once we were home, the bone in my arm healed and my shoulder responded well to physiotherapy and returned to full mobility. Tony started having physiotherapy but it made little or no difference and he was sent for an MRI scan which showed that he had a bulging disc in his spine that was pressing on his spinal cord. Shortly afterwards he went into hospital to have the bulging disc trimmed and his spine decompressed. The Lord had said that He would heal him through the surgeon and praise the Lord, when he came out of surgery, the pains in his legs were gone!

We could have been tempted to blame the enemy for all these things, but the Lord spoke to us and said:

"These things you have gone through are the door through which you will enter into greater things. You will do the 'bigger things' I have promised."

"For my thoughts are not your thoughts, neither are your ways my ways," declares the LORD. Isaiah 55:8

How unsearchable His judgements, and His paths beyond tracing out! Who has known the mind of the Lord? Romans 11:33-34

Chapter 19

Mount Moriah Trust 2018 – 2020

2018

As if we did not have troubles enough, in January we had to deal with criminals using the Trust's website to test the validity of credit card data that they had stolen. They made 19,700 transactions over three days and we had to individually refund over eight hundred fraudulent transactions that went through. Thankfully the vast majority were blocked as the cards were no longer valid.

Apparently this is a common practice. Criminals who have stolen credit card data need a way in which they can check which accounts are still valid and have funds. They do this by finding a website, often a charity website, that accepts donations. They start with a few manual transactions then use an automated process to make thousands of small transactions of £5 or $5. If the transaction is accepted they know that the card is still active and has funds.

Needless to say, we had to implement changes to the website to stop this happening again. Even today we can see that criminals have tested our process with some small transactions and it is reassuring to know that our system is robust enough to spot and reject them.

Zechariah Arni the pastor of the Ethiopian Messianic Retzon HaEl Congregation in Haifa had a bad car accident in June. The Lord had protected Zechariah physically and he was unhurt but his car was a write-off. Although he would receive some money from the insurance company there was no way that he could afford to make up the difference for another car. As having a car was such an important part of being able to fulfil his pastoral work within his community, the Trust launched a fund to help him. The Lord provided by touching hearts across the world and in July we were able to send a considerable sum which enabled him to purchase a new (used) car.

Every so often the Lord gives us the most wonderful surprises. In our Monthly Prayer letter for May-June we included the following prayer requests from Pastor Nizar Toumah, Church of the Nazarene in Nazareth:

> Our pre-school opened in the early eighties to provide local children with a Christian education and a strong base in the Word of God without discrimination of religion or background. The school needs maintenance and upgrading of classrooms and the playground.
> - Pray for strength and energy as we both serve in the church and the pre-school.
> - Wisdom as we deal with parents from different backgrounds and beliefs (half the children are from Muslim families).
> - Pray for God's provision for the financial needs of the Pre-school.
> - Pray for protection for our family.
> - Pray for sponsors to help the children of poor families that cannot afford the full fee.

The last of these prayer requests touched the hearts of a family in Singapore who provided a very generous gift to sponsor a number of children from poor Christian families to attend the pre-school for the year that started in September. It was so inspiring and encouraging to see how answers to prayer like this were impacting lives.

Our annual visit to Israel was hectic as we tried to make up for missing so many appointments in 2017 when I broke my arm. We had fifty-seven meetings in forty-two days and travelled from Eilat in the South to Nahariyya in the North. It was quite an effort but thanks to the Lord we were able to meet or speak on the phone to all the Pastors and leaders with whom we work. We also met some new pastors who had been recommended to us to hear about their needs and prayerfully consider providing them with support.

It was good to catch up with the pastors and congregations in the centre and south of the country and we travelled down to Eilat to meet Pastor Ariel Ben-David for the first time and attended the Shabbat meeting of the HaMaayan Eilat Congregation. We were fortunate to get out of Eilat the next morning before rains of Biblical proportions flooded the town making roads impassable and submerging cars in underground car parks. Thank you Lord!

So many of the congregations in the Land were struggling with their finances. Harassment and persecution of the Messianic Jewish community by the ultra-Orthodox was increasing. The message we received from so many pastors was that "the needs are great but the resources are lacking". We had many requests to increase our regular support or provide additional funds for specific needs, many of which were heart rending.

We would love to have been able to instantly say "yes" to these requests but the reality was that for the past few months the Trust had been struggling to meet its existing commitments. It had been a testing time but the Lord had been faithful and when things had seemed almost hopeless He came through with a big donation out of the blue. We were so grateful for our faithful supporters.

However, if the Lord wanted us to continue providing support at the same level and especially if we were to continue to grow, we needed to increase our support base. We were praying that the Lord would touch hearts and provide new supporters. We needed the Lord to open new doors for us in the UK and overseas so that we could reach new audiences. We prayed that during our upcoming visit to Malaysia, Australia and Singapore He would open many new doors that would lead to new supporters and new sources of finance.

2019

2019 was a year of consolidation, sadly we were unable to take on any of the new commitments that we had discussed during our 2018 visit due to financial constraints. We continued to meet our existing commitments up until November but after that we had to reduce them slightly to balance the books. As this is the Lord's work and He is Jehovah Jireh, the Provider, He had a purpose in what he was doing. Since that time the Lord has balanced our books and we have not had to make further adjustments.

We did not visit Israel in 2019 as the Lord had other plans for us with our home church. We were in regular touch with all the pastors by telephone and e-mail, something that would become standard practice in 2020 due to the Covid-19 virus.

2020

As I write this book, the Trust's eighteenth year of operation has just concluded. The Trust supports twenty-three Messianic Jewish Pastors and Congregations and Lech L'cha the youth ministry, plus nine Christian Arab Pastors and Congregations, the House of Light Social Aid Ministry and two Christian Arab children's homes.

On the occasion of the Trust's 18th Birthday we received this tribute from Jay Rawlings and family in Jerusalem:

> Congratulations on reaching the 18th Anniversary of Mount Moriah Trust.
>
> Your outstanding, life filled, service to the servants of the Lord here in the Holy Land is certainly timely and valued. You have been like a Mother and a Dad to many, many people here. As the Apostle Paul said, *"there are many teachers but few fathers!"* Corinthians 4:15
>
> You have helped many of us in times of need by the blessing of the Lord working through you both in selfless and quiet

Godly ways. Thank you for listening and acting, thus creating fruit that only one day will be revealed. In our fifty years of serving the Lord via the media in Israel we have never met more sincere, humble and Godly saints who never look for praise nor acknowledgement only "the Heart of God" at work in His people in His Land."

"Ad maya vey esrim," May you continue on for at least another 120 years.

Sincerely,

Jay, Meridel, David, Chris, Josh and Daniel Rawlings

During the year the Trust passed the significant financial milestone of having sent over £1.5 Million to the needy in God's Land. We thank God for His faithful provision!

Milestones passed in God's Provision to the needy in His Land

Milestone	year	year	year	year	year	year
£1,500,000						2020
£1,250,000					2018	
£1,000,000				2016		
£750,000			2014			
£500,000		2011				
£250,000	2008					
Time taken	6 years	9 years	12 years	14 years	16 years	18 years

LORD, all that we have accomplished you have done for us. Isaiah 26:12

The Covid-19 pandemic has hit Israel very badly. The country went from record numbers of tourists to no tourists almost overnight. By September over 1 million people had lost their jobs and over 30,000 small businesses had ceased to operate.

The virus itself was spreading rapidly and a new national lockdown was ordered from 25th September. Prime Minister Binyamin Netanyahu issued a special statement to the nation on 24th September in preparation for the tightening of the lockdown restrictions the next day. After expressing appreciation for the dedication of health personnel and citizens who lend a hand to others in need, he said: "These lockdown measures are not easy, but saving lives comes first. This is a national emergency. We are at the height of an ongoing war – the Corona War. The entire world is in the throes of the pandemic. The plague is also expected, unfortunately, to take an additional heavy toll in human lives. I am sorry but this is the truth," Netanyahu said. "There is one simple rule – when you open up the economy, the morbidity goes up. Unfortunately, with the removal of the restrictions, there is a gradual slackening in adherence to health regulations.

(INN / VFI News)

Defence Minister Benny Gantz also issued a statement on the same evening. "We are in one of the most difficult crises we have ever known. We are fighting for the lives of the citizens of Israel. I refuse to be drawn into populism, obsessions, or cynicism, but instead to focus on saving lives and saving society," Gantz said. "The decision to open the economy was too early, the decision to transfer the responsibility for cutting off the chain of infection to the IDF came too late," "This is not a struggle between protesters and worshipers, this is not a virus that only affects the Haredim or secular. This is a war for our lives." (INN / VFI News)

We see God's hand over the Trust and over this book. The Trust was born in 2002 at a time of economic distress and mass unemployment caused by the Second Intifada. This book is being birthed at a time of economic distress and mass unemployment caused by the covid-19 pandemic.

The outcome and outreach are unknown to us but God has His

plans for His work to proceed in His way, in His good and perfect timing, for His purposes and plans to be fulfilled.

We are unable to travel to promote the work and probably will not be able to do so for some considerable time. We are praying that God will use this book to do the travelling for us, touching hearts to join Him in His work.

Yes and Amen to all that He is doing. Praise His Glorious Name.

Chapter 20

God's Appointed Times

*There is a time for everything, and a season for every
activity under the heavens.* Ecclesiastes 3:1

God hates grumblers! Take a look at the grumbling Israelites in
the wilderness when He miraculously took them out of Egypt and
provided for them.

In 2005 I found myself grumbling to God, bemoaning the fact that
I had no relatives left, all my immediate family had died.

We had been a small family anyway. I was an only child. Tony and
I had chosen not to have any children. There were not many aunts,
uncles or cousins. So now I felt bereft of close relatives.

The Lord rebuked me. He said: *"I have given you many Jewish
families."* Mortified by my grumbling, I humbly said how sorry I was
and thanked Him for His gracious loving kindness. Tony and I were
so blessed by all the families we had met in Israel.

But God's grace is infinite and boundless. Three months later, we
received a letter, out of the blue, from a cousin in Australia. Margaret
(Marg) and her husband Don were visiting the UK and wondered if
we could meet. I had known her brother Jim really well. He had left
Australia and come to live and work in the UK many years before. He
often came to stay with my Mum and Dad, and it was through Jim
that I met Tony. They both worked for BOAC, later to become British
Airways. He then returned to Australia and we didn't have very

much contact. I knew he had a sister but there had been no contact whatsoever. But in God's timing, all that was about to change. Marg and Don came to stay for a couple of nights at the end of their tour to Europe and the UK.

We all got on so well and there was the added bonus that we were all Christians. We knew the Lord had brought us together. We enjoyed the time we spent in each other's company and they invited us to visit them in Tamworth, New South Wales. I was so overwhelmed by the Lord's forgiveness and goodness. Despite my ungracious grumbling, in His infinite mercy and kindness, He had brought members of my family from the other side of the world!

It was like having the sister I had never had. Marg wished we had met sooner, but it was God's time for us to meet. Everything awaits His 'appointed time'. And so began our trips to Australia every two years. The Lord works on so many different levels. He had a plan not only to bless us with family, but to begin the work of the Mount Moriah Trust in Australia.

The Great South Land of the Holy Spirit

Through this special family He had so graciously given us to enjoy, He was about to enlarge the work in the great continent of Australia; 'the Great South Land of the Holy Spirit'. These are the words of Captain Pedro Fernandez de Quiros in 1606, explorer and missionary, who had discovered the great southern landmass. He was a Catholic Jew who was burdened with a desire to establish a holy settlement to be called 'The New Jerusalem'.

On the Day of Pentecost, 14 May 1606, he declared:

> "Let the Heavens, the earth, the waters with all their creatures and all those present witness that I, Captain Pedro Fernandez de Quiros… in the Name of Jesus Christ… hoist this emblem for the Holy Cross on which His [Jesus Christ's] person was crucified and whereon He gave His life for the ransom and

remedy of all the human race... on this Day of Pentecost, 14 May 1606... I take possession of all this part of the South as far as the pole in the Name of Jesus... which from now on shall be called the Southern Land of the Holy Ghost."

An honour bestowed on no other nation! A prophetic proclamation all those years ago.

The work in Australia was soon to begin!

Chapter 21

The Supporters

Whatever You have commanded us we will do,
and wherever You send us we will go. Joshua 1:16

We praise God for the supporters! They are absolute treasures. Where would we be without them? There would certainly be no Trust without their loving, faithful giving and prayers. They are the Trust, chosen vessels of the Lord Himself. He said that:

"My Holy Spirit will touch hearts to give."

Every time we receive a donation, we know it is the work of the Lord, a gift from His Hand through His chosen ones. We are always totally amazed because the Lord has said to us we are only to ask Him for what we need. Therefore, we do not fundraise, and we do not write letters asking for money. We tell people that there are needs and leave the rest to Him. Sometimes we wonder where and how we have received all the gifts; it is the miraculous provision of God! We visit the pastors and leaders each year and discuss with them their needs and decide with them who needs help and how much we will give. We make a covenant to provide each month for the coming year. We do this without knowing that the finances will be available during that time. In this way we are a Faith Ministry. We never have a fund of money from which to work, because the Lord said: *"Give out what you have."*

It is just like Jesus feeding the five thousand. There were only five loaves and two fish to feed everyone, but as the disciples gave out what they had, there was a supernatural multiplication and everyone ate and had enough. In fact there were twelve baskets of leftovers (Matthew 14:13–21). The Lord has given us this same principle to work from and He provides supernaturally. Hence the logo He gave us for the Trust, the loaves and the fish.

It is also like the little flour and oil that the widow of Zarephath had and the Lord, through Elijah, kept multiplying it during the years of famine (1 Kings 17:7–16). This is how the Trust operates. The Lord has always supplied the finance for us to give what we have covenanted to give to the Fellowships and families. The channel He uses to do this is the supporters.

By His grace and loving kindness we have so far been able to give over £1.5 million to believers in need in Israel, Gaza and the West Bank.

We give Him our praise and thanksgiving for His supernatural provision and His faithfulness to all His promises.

The Trust's support base in the UK has grown slowly and largely by word of mouth and more effectively by recommendation. The Trust is not a big or well-known name that immediately opens doors for us to speak about the work. We have found churches and pastors reluctant, with good reason, to invite us to speak without the recommendation of someone they know and trust. We have been fortunate to have Ken Burnett and Pastor John Angliss among others whose word has been trusted enough to get us an invitation. Word of mouth has been successful with many Israel focussed groups within the UK, but we pray that more doors would open to give us the opportunity to share about God's work. Without more supporters we will not be able to grow and expand the work in God's Land.

One of the most important developments in our growth was the expansion overseas. Meeting my cousin Marg and her husband Don in the UK in 2005 provided the spur to visit them in Australia in 2006/2007. Ken Burnett encouraged us to visit Patrick and Joan

Sheehan, the Prayer For Israel (PFI) representatives in Brisbane. They took us to meet Richard and Shirley Jones, PFI members in Toowoomba. We explained to them all about the Trust and were invited to speak about the work when we next visited in 2009. The seeds for expansion into Australia had been sown!

Reading *The Elijah Legacy* by David Davis, I saw that the Foreword was written by Noel Mann, the Senior Pastor of Zion Christian Ministries in Brisbane, Australia. It was as if the Lord highlighted the name Noel Mann and I felt we should meet him on our next visit.

In 2009 we gave our first Australian presentations to PFI groups in Brisbane and Toowoomba. We met Pastor Noel Mann and were invited to speak to a prayer group from Zion Ministries in Brisbane. Wow! What an amazing experience to meet Noel and share with this wonderful, passionate, Spirit led group. It was quite a night, very hot and humid, with God moving mightily both inside and outside the building. A terrific thunderstorm started during the meeting and continued long into the night. On our journey back to our hotel in Broadbeach the rain was so heavy we could hardly see in front of us to drive, but the Lord saw us safely back. What a night in so many ways! It was the beginning of a very blessed relationship with Zion Christian Ministries.

During 2008 we gave a presentation to the "4Israel" group in Kent. Rosemary Cheshire, one of the ladies at the meeting, was from Australia and told us about 'Shalom Israel' run by Pat Ramsay in Melbourne, who she thought would be interested in our Ministry.

Whilst we were in New South Wales, Tony rang Pat to explain who we were. We were a little worried about cold calling her as these calls were rarely successful. But unknown to us at the time, this was one of the Lord's Divine Appointments. The friendship with Pat and our association with Shalom Israel hugely increased the Trust's outreach in Victoria and other States across Australia. Our relationship with Pat and Shalom Israel has deepened and grown over the years and we praise the Lord for bringing us together. I will let Pat explain the beginning of our alliance together:

Connecting with Mount Moriah Trust was a divine appointment for our ministry. Shalom Israel was birthed in February 1991. Our aim was to be a teaching ministry to the church on God's purposes for Israel and the Jewish people. We are a non-profit organisation. We held regular seminars with well-known overseas and local speakers on God's purposes for Israel and opening up to us the teaching on our Hebraic roots.

For many years we donated our proceeds to various Jewish groups here in Melbourne to be sent to their organisations in Israel, as well as supporting a couple of Christian ministries helping Jewish needs within Israel.

The scripture we used was Romans 15:27 *For if the Gentiles have shared the Jew's spiritual blessings, they owe it to the Jews to share with them their material blessings.*

Lindsay and Martha Bear who were co-founders with myself for Shalom Israel had gone to be with the Lord in 2000 and 2002 respectively.

For some time, I had been thinking about that verse (Romans 15:27) wondering how we could bless the Jewish believers through our material possessions.

ANSWER – January 2009 The Divine Appointment

In January 2009 I received a call from Tony and Kathy who were visiting in Australia asking me if they could share the work of The Mount Moriah Trust. I asked them to send me some of their material and we would pray about it and call them back.

I was drawn immediately to this work and asked them if they could visit Melbourne and we would have them speak at a local church hall and share their ministry.

So February 5th 2009 in a rented hall Tony and Kathy shared their work of the Mount Moriah Trust. As usual, the enemy tried to put a spoke in the works through the equipment. After forty minutes in the middle of the Powerpoint presentation everything went black and stopped. We adjourned for a cup of tea (what else?). It transpired that their laptop was plugged into a power socket that was not connected to the electricity! We found a new socket that did have power and the meeting continued uneventfully to the end.

This was the beginning of a partnership that has continued to blossom over the last eleven years. One of the key points presented was that every cent given in a donation went to the believers in the land. Tony and Kathy were covering all expenses themselves which included all travel wherever they went. Since that time our donations and profits from all sales have increased, knowing what better place to give but the pastors and congregations in the land, who were able to take the gospel to their own people.

It is such a joy now to have regular updates and testimonies from the body of believers in the land, truly fulfilling Paul's words of Romans 15:27. We love getting updated DVDs and seeing the Jewish and Arab believers giving their testimonies of the ways that God's provision through MMT has made a difference. Tony and Kathy visit these congregations each year. In these last days I can't think of a better way to give than to MMT as we may be restricted in visiting the land in the future, but our donations are being used by those that are reaching out to their own taking the miracle message of salvation.

Pat Ramsay, Co-Founder, Shalom Israel Melbourne Australia.

On our way home from Australia we stopped in Hong Kong for a week and met up with Gloria Mok from God's Glory Ministry. What a blessing Gloria was! She produced leaflets and flyers in English and Chinese before our arrival and introduced us to Pastor David Ho who invited us to give our presentation at his Sunday church service.

We also spoke to a group of Christian ladies with a heart for Israel. In seven days we gave five presentations, each translated into Chinese, to about 130 people many of whom were visiting from the Chinese mainland. The response was amazing and it was so good to learn that the Chinese understand the place of Israel in God's heart.

In 2011 the Lord mightily blessed our ministry tour of Australia. Our hosts made us extremely welcome as we made presentations in Brisbane, Toowoomba, Perth, Adelaide, Melbourne and Sydney including an invitation from Rev. Gordon Moyes to speak in NSW Parliament House. The Lord had opened new doors to new groups and churches. The Shalom Israel seminar was the highlight of our tour.

The response was overwhelming at times as the Lord touched so many hearts to join in His work. We were amazed at the generosity of the gifts for the needy believers and the wonderful prayer that we received for the work. Again we stopped in Hong Kong on the way home and Gloria Mok hosted a presentation and did a wonderful job translating into Chinese – including the sound track of the DVD!

We praise and thank the Lord for the wonderful time He gave us in January and February 2013 touring New South Wales, Queensland and Victoria presenting the work of MMT. He gave us a time of great rest and recuperation in January followed by ten presentations during February. As well as being able to update old friends/congregations the Lord opened doors to a number of new congregations. We were truly blessed by the reception we were given, the way people embraced the work of MMT and by the amazing generosity of everyone we met. Our special thanks went to Pat Ramsay for the fund-raising activities on MMT's behalf and for the amazing gift at the end of the Shalom Israel Seminar in Melbourne.

This time we stopped in Singapore on our way home and gave five presentations in the seven days that we were there. Again the Lord opened new doors and sowed seeds for the future. There were two divine appointments that were to bless the Trust for years to come.

Nethanel and Tabitha Lam and Cyril Seah are special people who have made introductions for us to speak and meet new groups each time we have been in Singapore. It has been a privilege to speak to the Full Gospel Business Men's meeting whenever we are in town. Wherever we went we found great understanding of Israel's place in God's end time plans and were encouraged by how generously they embraced MMT's work.

Whilst in Israel in 2014 we had been invited by Julie Roche of Shekinah Tours, whom we had met at a Shalom Israel meeting in Melbourne, to speak to her tour group at their hotel just outside Jerusalem. Most of those we spoke to were from Malaysia and at the end of the evening they gave us a very generous gift. Brother Silas Seenivasagam told us that he had asked the Lord's guidance and the Lord had told him to: "Trust them." He invited us to visit them in Malaysia when we next went to the Far East.

So on our way to Australia in 2015 we stopped in Singapore and took the short flight across to Kuala Lumpur. We based ourselves in Klang, a city about one hour west of Kuala Lumpur. Pastor Albert Ong and Brother Silas Seenivasagam arranged for us to speak to Church Congregations, Full Gospel Business Men's meetings, the Klang Pastors' meeting and House groups. We visited Pastor Albert & YM Ong's amazing "Good Samaritan" Children's Home and The Boaz Field Drug and Alcohol Rehabilitation Centre where we gave a message of "God's love for the lost".

We received such a wonderful reception and hospitality from everyone we met, in fact if it had been the Lord Himself, He would not have been received better. The Body of Christ in Malaysia is under great pressure and harassment not least from the government. The government were making it difficult for Christians to visit Israel even on organized tours. Our brothers and sisters in Christ in Malaysia needed and still today need our prayers for their wellbeing.

In Singapore we rejoiced in the Lord's goodness. We spoke to Church congregations, a Full Gospel Business Men's Fellowship meeting, prayer groups and cell groups. Cyril Seah blessed us with his hospitality and fellowship and arranged meetings for us. It was part of God's plan for us to be in Singapore at the time. Cyril's wife Roslyn was diagnosed with breast cancer whilst he was away on a business trip and He used us to provide comfort and ministry to her. (Subsequently Roslyn's treatment was successful praise God!) We were greatly encouraged to be told by a pastor we met that "we walk in the supernatural by our faith in God as our provider."

In Australia as well as visiting many old friends in Queensland, Victoria and New South Wales, we met new groups in Cessnock, Moruya and Gerringong in NSW and Caulfield, Glen Waverley and New Gisborne in Victoria. The Shalom Israel Seminar in Melbourne attended by over two hundred people was, as always, a highlight and a delight for us to share what the Lord had been doing in the two years since we were last in Australia. We thanked and praised the Lord for Pat Ramsay and Enoch Lavender of Shalom Israel and for the strong partnership that had developed between us that was enabling the Trust to grow its work in God's Land.

So many times people said to us that hearing about the work of MMT was *"the answer to prayer as they had wanted to bless Israel but did not know how they could do it"*.

It was a very special trip and we were so grateful for the wonderful hospitality that we received wherever we went. The Lord rewarded us for our efforts, it was a blessed trip in every way, He even arranged for us to be upgraded to Business Class on three out of the four long-haul flights: London to Singapore, Singapore to Sydney and Sydney to Singapore. What a wonderful God we serve!

Before we left home for our visit to Malaysia, Australia and Singapore in 2016-2017, the Lord spoke to me and told me that He wanted us to speak about the Biblical basis for the work of MMT. We prepared a series of PowerPoint slides to remind people how God looks on Israel and the Jews, why we should pray for them, the debt we owe to the Jews and why we should support them today.

We gave eight presentations in Malaysia and it was so good to meet old friends and new pastors and their congregations. Christians in

Malaysia have a hard time from the Muslims and from the government and we needed the Lord's protection from enemy attack whilst we were there.

Praise the Lord for his protecting angels! One Sunday, Tony and I were standing at the top of the steps at the entrance to the Premiere Hotel waiting to be picked up to go to a church to give a message. Without any warning and for no reason I started to fall over sideways as though I had been pushed. My fall onto the lowest step took such a long time. Tony's impression was that it was so slow it was as if I was being cradled down. It had to be an angel letting me down gently! Tony noticed that I did not put my arm out to save myself as one would do normally, my arm stayed by my side as if it was being held there. I landed gently on the step and the only sign of my fall was a tiny graze on my shoulder, other than that I was completely unhurt. Whilst falling I felt that everything was happening in slow motion and I was asking myself "when am I going to land?" We knew that the Lord was with us!

However, the enemy did manage to get back at us just as we were leaving. At Kuala Lumpur airport, whilst checking-in for our flight to Singapore we had our camera and some money stolen from our hand luggage. At the time, the Lord did try to warn us but we did not recognise the danger He was warning us about. The biggest regret was losing the pictorial record of everything that we had done – a lesson to download our photos more regularly to our PC. Once in Australia, the Lord used the incident for good as we were able to replace our camera with the latest model which incorporated new functions and an improved technical specification!

We spent Christmas in Mandurah south of Perth, Australia. We had never been there before, so went out looking for a church to go to on Christmas Eve/Day. The Lord led us to The Lighthouse Apostolic Church and to some very special Pastors – Dennis and Wilfred. We were made so welcome, invited to share about MMT at a midweek meeting and to spend New Year's Eve with the church. This was the first of three unexpected "lighthouses" the Lord took us to in Australia.

The second was in Adelaide where we were booked to speak at

a prayer meeting which we found was to be held in the Adelaide Lighthouse Prayer Tower. The third came in Melbourne when we were invited to speak to the Lighthouse Christian College in Cranbourne south of Melbourne. What a privilege it was to speak to the eight hundred and fifty students and a hundred staff.

What is a lighthouse? It can be a warning of danger to be avoided but it can also be a means of showing the correct pathway to a safe harbour. We were certain that this was confirmation from the Lord that He wanted people to hear about the right path to be followed regarding Israel and the Jews.

He was using us, in a small way, to be a lighthouse showing the right path. We started every presentation in Malaysia, Australia and Singapore with this message and everywhere we went people used their phones to take photographs of the slides. Pastors also asked for copies of the presentation so that they could follow up the message in later services.

We gave twenty-four presentations in Australia and there were the usual enemy attacks through the audio/visual equipment, but we were always able to give our presentation despite the enemy's best/worst efforts.

In 2018-2019 we visited Malaysia, Australia and Singapore talking to an expanding number of churches and prayer groups. In Malaysia we ran a "Focus on Israel" seminar for pastors. Our ministry has now been firmly established in each of these countries but of course we wait for the Lord to open new doors to new audiences. Speaking to Churches and church groups in Singapore had become more difficult after a visiting overseas pastor said some injudicious things which caused problems.

The fruitfulness of these overseas relationships was demonstrated during the financial year which ended on 31st May 2019. For the first time we had received more donations from overseas (59%) than from the UK (41%). Our donations from Australia alone exceeded those from the UK.

We continue to be ready to go anywhere in the world that the

Lord sends us. In the early days we thought He would send us west to America but instead He sent us east. We would love Him to open new doors into new countries but we await His perfect timing. Now with the Covid-19 virus who knows when it will be safe to travel the world again? It is not possible to make any forward plans to visit Israel or the Far East. We would normally be planning to visit Australia in January/February 2021 but only God knows if this will be possible.

The Trust cannot thank the Lord enough for the amazingly generous group of supporters that He has given us. They uplift our brothers and sisters in God's Land both financially and spiritually and none of the work would have been possible without Him touching hearts to join Him in His work. We are so grateful!

Chapter 22

A Ministry of Encouragement

Encourage one another and build each other up.
1 Thessalonians. 5:11

What an important Ministry. God shows how important it is in His Word, the Bible. We see Jonathan encouraging David, standing by as a true friend when his life was threatened by Jonathan's father, King Saul. David could trust Jonathan –

Jonathan became one in spirit with David, and he loved him as himself… Jonathan made a **covenant** *with David because he loved him as himself.* 1 Samuel 18:1,3.

The Mount Moriah Trust stands as a true friend to the Jews, Arabs and Palestinians in God's Land; the "One New Man in Christ". We stand alongside the believers in prayer and finance, helping them in their time of need when their lives become difficult. We have a **covenant** relationship with the Pastors, Fellowships and Leaders and give them help on a regular basis. We serve them *"shoulder to shoulder"*. Zephaniah 3:9.

Pastor Tal gave us a word from the Lord on 11th November 2011:

"I have made a Covenant with you."

Ken Burnett our Patron wrote the article that follows for our April 2005 Newsletter describing the Trust as an "Aaron & Hur Ministry" supporting believers, God's spiritual army, in the front line of spiritual warfare in Israel.

The Mount Moriah Trust is an "Aaron and Hur" ministry

An article about Intercession by Ken Burnett

"But Moses' hands were heavy … and Aaron and Hur supported his hands. Thus his hands were steady until the sun set." (Exodus 17:12)

Here is intercession! Intercession at the height of the battle! And with priceless guidelines.

1. The context is the grumbling of the Israelites. (*"Is the Lord among us or not?"*) This gave spiritual opportunity to Israel's traditional adversary, and Amalek was soon there! (Exodus 17:8/9)
2. Even though Moses was there with God's authority (*the staff of God in his hand*) in the right place at the forefront, he grew weary. As long as he could hold up his hands the battle went well, but when he lowered his hands in weariness, the enemy Amalek prevailed.
3. This is one of the first and most lucid lessons on intercession in the Bible. "Scripture teaches here that, when the Israelites looked up to God and humbled themselves, they were victorious. But when they did not, they were defeated." (*Dr J Hertz – Soncino Press*)
   a) It was the top leadership in particular (Moses) that grew weary and needed support.
   b) The Spirit here **calls not one, but two persons to support, and both were priests.** The spiritual (prayer) principle here is of utmost importance and should be heeded. (Ecclesiastes 4:9/10; and Matthew 18:20)
   c) Every muscle in Aaron's and Hur's bodies is stretched and taut. True intercession can be costly at times. (Romans 8:26; 12:1)
   d) Moses could not fall over; Aaron was on one side and Hur was on the other.

e) *"They took a stone and put it under him, and he sat on it."* This is the tested stone, the costly stone, the Foundation Stone, Jesus – of Isaiah 28:16. It is the prayer of faith bringing the leader to the place of rest and faith. *"and Moses __sat__ on it."*

f) *"Thus, his hands were steady (Hebrew "of faith") until the sun set."* The little word *"Thus"* here virtually says: *In this way, (as a direct result of all that Aaron and Hur did) stability came!*

4. *The Mount Moriah Trust is an" Aaron and Hur" ministry,* in the sense of supporting believers (who are God's spiritual army) in the front line of spiritual warfare in Israel. Satan's efforts to annihilate the Jewish people have not ceased since their Exodus from Egypt in 1500BC!

But the Bible tells us that *one day His glory will be seen* upon that nation! (Isaiah 60:1/3)

Pastor Dimitri Brodkin in his contribution to the "Heart of God" video made in 2009 also likened the work of the Trust to that of Aaron and Hur. He said:

"In the Bible we see how Moses had to keep his arms raised for victory. It was very hard. Aaron and Hur stood by supporting him with his hands raised. This is what we see here, the Mount Moriah Trust supporting us like Aaron and Hur. These poor people attending the Grace House Soup Kitchen thank God for all that Mount Moriah Trust does. They pray for you because they ask that God will bless you because you help them."

Elisha served Elijah and stood alongside him for ten years until Elijah was taken up into God's Presence. Elisha was his helper and faithful companion to the elderly prophet. God put them together in the time of Elijah's discouragement and weariness to help him through a difficult time, to encourage him.

Barnabas encouraged many in the early church and helped the apostle Paul become established in his ministry, standing alongside him and assisting him in teaching great numbers of people. Acts 11:23,25,26.

Although the ministry of encouragement may seem like a minor gift or a lesser calling, the most important thing is whether you are faithful to God's calling on your life.

We are all called to serve and encourage the believers in Israel, Gaza and the West Bank as they are precious in the Lord's sight. They all suffer persecution, experience hardship and difficulties financially and need our help and support. We need to be faithful to serve, quick to encourage, persevering in prayer.

Chapter 23

Prejudice

For there is no difference between Jew and Gentile
– the same Lord is Lord of all. Romans 10:12

Israel, Gaza, the West Bank, Jews, Arabs, Palestinians. What do these words stir within you?

One thing is for certain, the Lord will **not** tolerate prejudice or bitterness of any kind. It always needs to be addressed and dealt with. In God's divine love there is no discrimination between race or position or gender *"for you are all one in Christ Jesus."* Galatians 3:26-28. *"God created mankind in his own image."* Genesis 1:27

Our lives are bombarded by world media, news, views and information abound, some correct and some not. We can be influenced by worldly values, government bias, racial extremists. We can see events through a political lens and our vision can become skewed.

This can happen with the way we think about the Jews, the Arabs in Israel and the Arabs in Gaza and the West Bank known generally as the Palestinians. If we are not careful, the news and political ideologies can affect our Christian thinking. We can take sides, even without our being aware of it.

On our travels we've met people, and Christians included, who have very entrenched views about the Jews, the Arabs, the Palestinians. Some love one, and dislike, even hate, the other. The Lord has told us to be balanced and not political in our dealings.

We need to check our eyesight, check the health of our heart, check whether our mind has been renewed – to come in line with the Lord. We need heart vision of the Almighty God, the King of creation, the lover of our souls.

> *For God **so** loved the **world** that He gave His One and only Son, that whoever believes in Him shall not perish but have eternal life."* John 3:16.

He created and loves all people. Jesus died for the reconciliation of all nations. Through Jesus's work on the cross, we have been made one in Christ – Jews and Gentiles. We are now the 'One New Man' – Jews, Arabs, Palestinians:

> *For He Himself is our peace, who has made the two one and has destroyed the barrier, the dividing wall of hostility, by abolishing in His flesh the law with its commandments and regulations. His purpose was to create in Himself **one new man** out of the two, thus making peace, and in His body to reconcile both of them to God through the cross, by which He put to death their hostility.* Ephesians 2:14–16.

We need to ask the Lord to search us, to root out any attitudes that are dishonouring, displeasing to Him, some we may not even be aware of – to bring us into line with the vast depths of His agape love.

> *Search me, O God, and know my heart; test me and know my anxious thoughts. See if there is any offensive way in me, and lead me in the way everlasting.* Psalm 139:23.

A powerful prayer, one that God loves to answer. So watch out!

Chapter 24

Greater Outreach:
Teaching from the Word of God

Each of you should use whatever gift you have received to serve others, as faithful stewards of God's grace in its various forms.
1 Peter 4:10

The Lord is so vast, His plans so extensive that we never know where He will direct us and for what purpose.

The Lord had often spoken to us from Isaiah 54:2-3;

Enlarge the place of your tent, stretch your tent curtains wide,
do not hold back, lengthen your cords, strengthen your stakes,
for you will spread out to the right and to the left.

We had assumed He was speaking about increasing the Fellowships and the families we support and increasing the outreach of the work into new areas and countries.

But God's vision is so much greater, so much deeper and bigger than we can imagine. We did not think that we would be giving Bible messages to Congregations in Israel to Jews and Arabs! Never 'assume' anything with the Lord. As we know it 'makes an ass of you and me'. His plans are much bigger than ours. We should never be surprised where God leads or what He asks us to do. He always provides for all that He wants to accomplish. Teaching from the Word of God has become a very important part of our work. He gives us the messages and the words. He provides the opportunities. He deals with the outcome and what is achieved. We just have to be willing. We just have to say, like Isaiah, *"Here am I. Send me!"* Isaiah 6:8.

From the beginning, Moshe was leading a house church in his home every Shabbat. When Tony and I visited Israel each year, we would enjoy a meal with his group and take part in the Bible studies. He asked if I would help him with the teaching. I asked the Lord if it was right for me to do this and He said I was to help them. So began a number of years of speaking to the group when we were in Israel and when back in England, I would prepare teaching tapes as the Lord directed and send them once a month. I love teaching from the Word of God. The teacher in me was 'resurrected' to do this and I felt privileged to teach the Lord's Jewish brothers and sisters from the Bible which is Jewish.

In those first years of the Ministry of the Trust, Moshe would drive us around Israel to meet the pastors and families. He stayed in the various hotels with us and got to know the pastors well. The three of us would visit the families in their homes, we would enjoy meals with the pastors and talk about the needs. Moshe was accepted as a friend and he was delighted as a Jew, to visit and eat in Arab homes. We saw the 'One New Man in Christ' taking place before our eyes. It was a very special time for all of us.

Staying in hotels gave us time for Bible study in hotel lobbies. I would prepare notes on a variety of subjects; basic Christian foundational teaching, characters from the Bible, the types of Christ, the life of Paul, the letters in the New Testament, the End Times, the Rapture, Tribulation, the Millennial Kingdom, the Plans and Purposes of Israel, their Destiny, the Marriage of the Lamb and so on.

On two of three occasions, Moshe and I were so aware of the Presence and Power of the Lord as we finished our time of study. It was the same experience that I had in the Tunnels at the Western Wall. We were both left dazed and weak from experiencing the Presence of Jesus. It would take a few minutes to recover as we sat quietly. It did not happen every time, but when it did it was memorable.

I could understand more easily how Daniel felt after the powerful heavenly visions he received of the End Times:

I, Daniel, was exhausted and lay ill for several days. Daniel 8:27

I had no strength left. Daniel 10:8

In 2007 early in our relationship with Pastor Hani and Shifa Billan and Cana Baptist Church we were enjoying fellowship in their home with their family one evening after the Sunday service when Sahar, Shifa's sister, asked if I would speak at the ladies' meeting at the Church. After praying about it, the Lord confirmed it was of Him and that was the beginning of my annual teaching when we visited Cana. It has been a delight and a privilege to meet with the ladies who are deeply committed to the Lord in their faithfulness and devotion.

In 2009 the Lord had given me a Bible study and teaching based on Mary of Bethany who sat at Jesus's feet and who ministered to Him a few days before His crucifixion anointing Him with pure nard from her alabaster jar (Matthew 26:6-13). Jesus spoke deeply to these ladies, telling them how much He loves them and that He wants them to spend more time sitting at His feet. It was a powerful message.

One of the women had gone home and told her husband about the message. The following week he brought his wife to the meeting and came in to thank me for the teaching! How wonderful to be the channel for the Lord's message to His people. Jesus said:

*I AM the vine; you are the branches... apart from Me **you can do nothing.*** John 15:5. [emphasis added].

In 2011, the Lord's message for the ladies was based on Derek Prince's *The Divine Exchange at the Cross and the Power of the Blood.* I prepared and gave to each of the ladies a booklet of notes which Pastor Saleem Hanna from Turan had translated into Arabic for me. The session was a great success and Shifa later used the notes to give the same message to the Youth Group in the Church at Easter.

In 2012, the Lord's message to the Ladies' group was a great encouragement to them. It featured Mary Magdalene, who was delivered of seven demons by Jesus and became His devoted follower. Jesus showed them how He honours women and holds them in high esteem.

In 2013, the message to the ladies was 'Bible promises to build your faith'. He wanted them to know in their hearts how they are His precious daughters and that He wants them to live knowing that they belong to Him and are His treasured possessions. The ladies praised God for His encouragement.

In 2014, the message was 'Mary of Nazareth, the mother of Jesus'. One of the ladies said at the end of the meeting that the message gave them fresh perspective and meaning about Mary and how necessary it was because of all the Mary worship in the Catholic churches. God confirmed by the comments and response that this had been His message. When Tony and Pastor Hani entered the hall at the end of the meeting they felt the Presence of the Lord very powerfully.

In 2015, Katy, the wife of Pastor Nizar Touma, of the Church of the Nazarene, in Nazareth invited me to give the same message about Mary of Nazareth to the ladies at their meeting.

The session went well and afterwards two or three women said how much they had learned. One woman said she really saw the meaning of Mary and how they must explain to others what the Bible says, not what the priests say about her. The Holy Spirit was present to teach and edify the ladies.

In 2016 the teaching in Cana was about Ruth and her faithfulness to Naomi, her Jewish mother-in-law. The teaching provoked a lively discussion at the end of the meeting about the genealogy showing the line through the men not the women and the Jewishness of the genealogy. They realised that Jesus and the apostles were Jewish. The ladies said they learned a lot and felt people needed to hear these things.

In 2017, the message was about 'Martha' and showed how *"she sat at Jesus's feet and also Mary"* (KJV) and how spiritual she was. She said to Jesus: *"I believe that You are the Christ (Messiah), the Son of God who was to come into the world."* John 11:27.

The only other person who said that to Jesus was Peter:

"You are the Christ (Messiah) the Son of the living God."
Matthew 16:16

Jesus spoke the amazing words to her: *"I AM the Resurrection and the Life"* (John 11:25) and then proved His words by raising her brother Lazarus from the dead.

The Lord set the ladies free from the negativity of being labelled 'Marthas'. They saw that Martha was not as unspiritual as they often heard she was.

That year (2017) the Lord extended the outreach to the Morning Star Fellowship in Tiberias and to the House of Light Ladies' Meeting in Shefar'am. The message to these groups was 'Mary of Bethany' and the following year, 2018 'Martha'.

How gracious the Lord is – He has enlarged the teaching to ladies' groups in Cana, Nazareth, Shefar'am and Tiberias. I have been very privileged to share studies that the Lord has given on Women in the Bible and to show what the Lord is saying to us. I am always amazed to see how the Lord uses these sessions to impact the lives of so many of the women and His timing in addressing issues in their lives.

Uplift and encourage My People

In 2009, Tony and I were humbled and very blessed by the Lord to convey messages of hope and encouragement to groups and church congregations in Israel – something we had never done before. Pastor Hani Billan invited us to speak to Cana Baptist Church. There is a dark spiritual climate around Cana and the believers are vastly outnumbered by the Muslims. The Lord wanted to remind them that

He can turn weakness into power and that, if they trust Him, He will make them all 'mighty warriors', like Gideon. The message uplifted and encouraged the young and the old in the Church.

Before we visited Pastor Tal Shiferaw's Beit El Kehilat in Jerusalem, we received a phone call from Tal saying that he and his wife Tigi felt the Lord had given us a message for the Church. We had not been expecting to speak at the meeting, but we realised the Lord wanted them to hear His 'army of Gideons' message that we had given to Cana Baptist Church. He knew that it would strengthen the courage and confidence of the brothers and sisters of this Ethiopian Messianic Congregation. The same message also blessed Moshe's Jerusalem House Church.

In 2012, Tony and I gave a message to the Church in Cana based on the 'Spiritual Blessings' we have in Christ, from Ephesians chapters 1 and 2. Again people were encouraged to hear the word. We gave the same message to Pastor Tal's congregation. The Lord uplifted and blessed them as they were reminded of His faithful promises.

In 2013, Israel Pochtar the pastor of the Beit Hallel Congregation in Ashdod, invited us to speak to a group of Russian Jewish believers and non-believers to explain to them why a Christian charity provides spiritual and financial support to the people of Israel. It was a great opportunity to share what the Bible says about Israel and the Jews:

> *For if the Gentiles have shared in the Jews' spiritual blessings, they owe it to the Jews to share with them their material blessings.* Romans 15:27

We explained what the spiritual blessings that we have received are and the plans that God has for Israel and the Jewish people. They were encouraged by the message.

Chapter 25

The Roots go deep

Have you not heard? Long ago I ordained it.
In days of old I planned it; now I have brought it to pass.
Isaiah 37:26

The roots of the Mount Moriah Trust go deep, deeper than I ever imagined.

One day as we visited the grave of my grandfather in Ramla, the Lord spoke an amazing word into my spirit: *"Your grandfather began the work of the Mount Moriah Trust."*

Staff Sergeant George Greig was a gunsmith and served in the First World War in Israel, called Palestine at that time.

He died in October 1918 of malaria and was buried in the Commonwealth War Graves Commission cemetery in Ramla. The country was full of malarial swamps and many soldiers died of malaria. He died six weeks before the end of the war. My grandmother was left a widow with four young children, my mother being the eldest at nine years of age. My grandmother had to survive on a war widow's pension which was very small. She struggled to bring up the children and if it hadn't been for the help of a relative in America, she would have been unable to cope. My mum, as was common in those days went out to work at fourteen, to help provide for the family.

The Lord was showing Tony and I at the graveside that after her husband's death my grandmother and her children were a poor family in need of help to survive. And now, nearly nine decades later George Greig's grand-daughter and her husband were being called to help poor and needy families in Israel the land where he had died!

What an amazing God! I had never seen this connection, but God saw it before it happened and knew that my grandfather's sacrifice had not been in vain, that the Lord would build on this foundation to bring about His purposes. God brings good out of every situation, even the sad and tragic events in life can be used to fulfil His eternal plans.

We were so humbled by the goodness and compassion of God, by His vastness in seeing the whole picture, His knowing the beginning and the end, His immensity way beyond our understanding. We were overawed by the realisation of His Greatness and Sovereign Power. We knelt at the graveside with tears of humility and gratitude to our great and mighty God.

The foundation of the Mount Moriah Trust went back a long way. It took sacrifice, pain and hardship, but was bringing forth a harvest of goodness and righteousness. The work of the Almighty God for His people in Israel, Gaza and the West Bank, the One New Man in Christ. What an incredible sovereign, loving God we serve!

Oh, the depth of the riches of the wisdom and knowledge of God! How unsearchable His judgements, and His paths beyond tracing out!... For from Him and through Him and to Him are all things. To HIM be the glory for ever! Amen. Romans 11:33,36

Tony and I are the only members of the family to have visited the grave. My grandmother had been given the chance to visit, but in those days the journey was long and she felt she could not leave her children. She died a couple of years before we had been to Israel and located the grave, but we were at least able to take photographs so that my mum could see her father's headstone. Her sister, my aunt, who was blind, enjoyed hearing about it as we described it to her.

We have never been able to find a lot of information about my grandfather's part in the war, where he served or where he died. We went to the Records Office in Kew and Tony had permission to search the records, but he discovered that many of the records had been destroyed in the Second World War when the building in London storing the records had been bombed. My grandfather's papers were among those destroyed and the only things that were left were small charred pieces of paper that gave us no information. His records were lost.

My grandmother had only received a telegram from the War Office informing her of his death from malaria. There was no information of any kind and she never received any of his personal belongings as they too were lost. But we cherish his memory and know that nothing is lost to God. He knows and sees everything.

Tony and I were actually in Israel on the 100th anniversary of his death on 18 October 2018 and were very moved to lay a wreath on his grave in memory of him.

The British Legion later sent a wooden cross to us to write a Tribute as part of the 2019 Fields of Remembrance. We wrote:

> Grandfather your sacrifice paved the way for the State of Israel and the Mount Moriah Trust. You are remembered with love and gratitude.

The British Legion wrote back:

> Your Tribute is a special one with its unique message. It stood proudly alongside over 100,000 others planted across six fields during this year's Remembrance. Thank you for being a part of such a special occasion and supporting the work of the British Legion.

Chapter 26

The Lord's work continues

Give thanks to the LORD and proclaim his greatness. Let the whole world know what he has done. 1 Chronicles 16:8 (NLT)

Publish his glorious deeds among the nations. Tell everyone about the amazing things he does. 1 Chronicles 16:24 (NLT)

So that is the story thus far of the Mount Moriah Trust. We pay tribute to the absolute faithfulness and trustworthiness of Almighty God to His promises and plans.

You know with all your heart and soul that not one of all the good promises the Lord your God gave you has failed. Every promise has been fulfilled; not one has failed. Joshua 23:14.

God is Sovereign but He has given us human responsibility in what He does. God will not do our part and we cannot do God's part. But together with God, we can do all that He asks us to do. We are co-workers with the Living, Almighty God, therefore:

We are more than conquerors. Romans 8:37

I can do everything through Him who gives me strength. Philippians 4:13

What a delight, an honour and a privilege to be co-workers with Him, the KING of the universe. It has been said: "We don't know what the future holds, but we know the One who holds our future."

When things have looked difficult, impossible even, He is the One who lifted our heads and our eyes to Him (*You lift up my head.* (Psalm 3:3); who whispered encouragement to continue and to run the race:

Run in such a way as to get the prize. 1 Corinthians 9:24

let us run with perseverance the race marked out for us. Hebrews 12:1.

Through our weakness, but in His strength, He leads us on in the knowledge that He is Faithful and True. The amazing timing of the Lord! As the worldwide Coronavirus (Co-vid 19) was beginning to take hold in the UK and lockdown was being enforced, the Lord quietly whispered:

"This is the time to write the story of the Mount Moriah Trust, to give Me the Glory for all that I have done for My People."

What a perfect time Confined at home with normal life on hold, everything cancelled, there was plenty of time to sit quietly with Him to write of His Goodness.

And as I looked at my history from the initial call of God as a fifteen year old teenager in 1960; the turning away from Him in abandonment; the many years of going my own way, of going astray until finally He called me back to fulfil His purposes and complete the Work He had planned from the beginning of time. I realised it was just like the history of Israel, His chosen people had abandoned their calling, but they too are coming back to their God, their Saviour, to the plan and purpose that Almighty God has always had for them. The amazing Grace of a Holy God!

I AM watching to see that My Word is fulfilled. Jeremiah 1:12

He who watches over you will not slumber; indeed, He who watches over Israel will neither slumber nor sleep. Psalm 121:3-4

We have yet to witness the end of the story!

The Lord calls us to continue. He walks out in front, we follow.

What a privilege and honour to serve our incredible God of Grace and Mercy and Lovingkindness. He is beyond our expectations. He is more than we will ever need. He is limitless, unfathomable, absolutely in control.

He is our Life, our Hope, our Future.

What a journey, what an adventure with the One who never fails, the Almighty Conqueror, the Victorious Coming King.

He is the One who says:

Have you not heard? Long ago I ordained it. In days of old I planned it; now I have brought it to pass... Isaiah 37:26

Do you not know? Have you not heard? Has it not been told you from the beginning? Have you not understood since the earth was founded? He sits enthroned above the circle of the earth... To whom will you compare Me? Or who is My equal? says the Holy One... The Lord is the everlasting God, The Creator of the ends of the earth. Isaiah 40:21-22,25,28

The Work continues...

It is unfinished like the book of Acts or an unfinished symphony. God's inexhaustible heart of love beats for those in need, for Jews and Gentiles, the ONE NEW MAN IN CHRIST.

"Do the work I have given you to do. I AM with you always."

Chapter 27

Pastors' Testimonies

We give thanks to You, O God. Psalm 75:1

When God told me to write this book, I wanted to give the Pastors the opportunity to give their testimonies of how the Lord has impacted the lives of believers in His Land through the Mount Moriah Trust. This chapter contains their testimonies and the testimonies of some of those who have personally received assistance.

Tony and I are not seeking any recognition through these testimonies but much as we might like the pastors to omit references to us, we know that it is inevitable that they mention our names because we are the "face" of the Trust and we are the people that deal with them and visit them. However, we are only doing the work the Lord has given us, to the best of our abilities and we thank Him for giving us this work. We might be the Chief Operating Officers of the Trust but He is the Chief Executive and we do what He tells us to do.

It was a pleasant surprise to see how many times Tony and I are referred to as a 'father and mother' to the families that the Trust has helped. The Lord has reconfirmed what He told me back in 2005 when I complained of having no family, He said that he had given us many Jewish and Arab families in His Land. We are truly blessed by this!

Pastor Nizar Touma, Church of the Nazarene, Nazareth

Mount Moriah is a name that has always brought joy to our lives and ministry. Your prayers and visits dear Tony and Kathy have impacted our lives in a very special way. The help and donations have always been like a cup of cold water to a thirsty soul and they will surely be rewarded by our Lord.

Friends we wouldn't be able to do what we did all these years without your help, drawing a beautiful smile on the face of a child, bringing joy to a sick man when we were able to buy him medicine or a poor family that received a package of food and we always told them that this was sent to you by some angel out there.

We surely appreciate your kindness and faithfulness all these years. You have always warmed our hearts with your generosity. We love you and pray for you.

Claude Ezagouri, Morning Star Fellowship, Tiberias

At the Morning Star Fellowship we are so grateful for the help for the needy that we received regularly from MMT. For some of our people it has been like oxygen as they would have never survived without this precious help. For example, I am thinking of a member of our fellowship who has to buy his monthly need of electricity. When the amount is over the power is cut off in his house and he and his family found themselves in darkness more than once. MMT gifts were a vital help for this family and their gratitude rises to heavens.

May the Lord, in His abundant grace, continue to provide the necessary funds to help God's people here on His promised land.

Yakov Dolinsky, Rock of My Salvation Congregation, Nazareth Illit

The Moriah Trust financial assistance found me at the right time. Being not a full-time minister and shepherding a Messianic Fellowship. I had to work at least a part time job. I had a job but with hours not sufficient to provide a necessary income for my family.

I understood that the Trust's offer of financial assistance was God's answer to my need. Receiving gifts on regular basis allows me to spend more time for the pastoral ministry. I still do a part time job but now I don't have to think how I am going to make both ends meet. Blessings!

Oded Shoshani, King of Kings Hebrew speaking congregation. Jerusalem

I thank the Lord for our many years of friendship and working together for Yeshua. We are deeply grateful for your faithful support in our Kehila. We wanted to send a few testimonies about how your support has blessed specific people in our Kehila:

A precious sister in our Kehila, L, is a single mother with two children. Her elderly mother who has health problems also lives with her. She has continued to faithfully work to support her family, but it is hard to make ends meet. For many years she also cleaned homes to bring in a bit extra. It was never enough though. She is a mighty prayer warrior and continues faithfully to pray and intercede for her family and the people who she works for. She is also sharing the Lord's love with many people. The Mount Moriah Trust's gifts allowed us to be able to support her on a monthly basis, and helped her to care for her family. The thing that I appreciate so much about this dear sister is her innocent delight and trust in the Lord.

She continues to steadfastly trust the Lord to supply for all of her needs and she rejoices, full of gratefulness, at the support that you have given. Thank you for walking together with her these last years!

Another mother in our Kehila has eight children. Her husband works, but the financial burden of such a large family is not an easy one. Additionally, beside the normal cost, there are extra expenses at the beginning of each school year to purchase supplies, books and uniform shirts. The mother also works in house cleaning and other manual labour, but she is unable to work full-time as her youngest is still not in kindergarten. The Mount Moriah Trust's support over the last number of years has been such a blessing, helping them to supply their children with the necessary things for school, and the dental treatments- such as braces that a few so desperately need. They are so grateful for the assistance that you have given, walking with them in support.

Pastor George Awad, ex-Director of the House of Hope, Bethlehem

I will never forget your prayers and support which helped the House of Hope to manage its vision to serve the Lord via serving the special needs children.

Ariel Ben-David, Hamaayan Eilat congregation, Eilat

I want to thank you for all support you did for us last years. It is very amazing, when people that even never see each other can be blessing, for me it is God's wonder! This is Lord's kindness and it gives me to be so thankful to Him and you as His ministers.

Hanna Massad, Christian Mission to Gaza

I want to express my deep gratitude for your generous support all these years to Gaza Baptist Church, through your program you helped the church pastor and the worship leader for many years with regular gifts plus helping others in the church on different occasions, thank you so much for your faithfulness, partnership and for standing with us all this time.

Shady El Najar – Worship Leader Gaza Baptist Church, Gaza City

Hello! My name Shady El Najar, and I was born in Gaza city and I live there still, with my wife, Raphada, and our two children. I have served in Gaza Baptist church for seventeen years. The Lord changed my life completely with His presence when I attended a church conference earlier in my life. After I accepted the Lord Jesus as my personal saviour, I knew God had called me into the ministry and my life would be His from then on. There were wonderful ministers, full of love and sincerity at this conference and God used them to show me how much He loved me, love all of us.

One of the Lord's servants at that time sat down and talked with me about our Lord Jesus, teaching me and answering all my questions. We decided to meet twice a week to study the Bible together, so I could learn and ask any questions I might have at the time. I also attended church on Sunday's and started to attend Christian conferences as often as I could. What encouraged me the most, was when I saw with my own eyes how much love Pastor Hanna Massad spread not only throughout the group of us in church, but also in the community. I saw this in Him, I saw God's love for us all through him, and through all of God's servants in the church. They all carried with them, wherever they went, the spirit of

215

His love. I started to experience on a more personal level how God can really come to live in our hearts. I was hungry for God and His word and started attending church regularly as well as helping with the youth meeting through the Awena Club.

I met my wife at a youth meeting, and I could see right away one of her most distinguishing features was her love for the Lord and her beautiful heart! God showed His love for me once again, by giving me Raphada! We got engaged and started to serve Him together in church. We led worship in church and saw God's Hand move in so many aspects of life. We received a lot of encouragement and support through the church and they continued to stand by us, counselling and advising, in many different situations.

As time went on, I had a bigger responsibility in this ministry. I worked with other leaders for the Awena Club and we grew together as a wonderful team, and family in the Lord. We felt God was always with us, never leaving or forsaking, even when we were feeling down. We spent a lot of time in prayer together seeking God's will for us, for the ministry and asking Him to help us in our weaknesses.

In life there are always tough times, and in Gaza we as believers know that all too well. We struggle financially, but the church has stood beside us and helped as much as they can. The political, economic, and social climate here in Gaza has always been exceedingly difficult and now more so than ever, in these uncertain times. What a blessing the support we receive from them, from you, has been. We thank the Lord daily for your love, care, and concern for us as your brothers and sisters in Christ.

You are always in our prayers and we want you to know how much we appreciate your love and support in the middle of the tough situations we (the Christian community in Gaza) often find ourselves in. We call Gaza home, and as hard as it is sometimes, God is ever faithful in our midst, after all He has sent us you, hasn't He?!

May the Lord bless and protect you, and once again thank you for standing with us in prayer, as well as financially. We could not do it without you!

Dov Bikas & Eduard Bitiev, Aviv Ministry, Tel Aviv

We are truly grateful to the Lord for you and your ministry! Your genuine care for our work and faithful support has been a great help and encouragement through the years. Your donations help us continue our outreach in Tel Aviv to the outcasts of the society – drug addicts, prostitutes and the homeless – and to bring them the Good News of God's love and salvation. You are also supporting the manager and coordinator of our work in Tel Aviv, Eduard Bitiev, who is doing a great, sacrificial job especially now, serving actively on the streets even though he belongs to a risk group as regards to coronavirus. Here is his personal letter to you:

Dear brothers and sisters! Dear not only because you are redeemed by the Blood of our Lord, but also because you are taking part in the life of our family so kindly. At this difficult time for all of us, when the whole world is seized by the fear of coronavirus, your donations help not only our family (my wife has been fired from work), but also our ministry. We understand that it is not easy for you to find these means, and therefore we want to encourage you with a passage from the Holy Scripture: *For God is not unrighteous to forget your work and labour of love, which ye have shewed toward his name, in that ye have ministered to the saints, and do minister* (Hebrews 6:10). We hug you with the Love of our Saviour Jesus Christ!

Howard & Randi Bass, Nachalat Yeshua congregation, Beersheva

It is hard to believe that it has been since 2002 that we have known each other, and that the Mount Moriah Trust has become part of God's blessings upon Yeshua's Inheritance Congregation in Beer Sheva! We truly thank the Lord for bringing us together, and that you both have become such a warm addition to our lives and arms of support. With fond memories of Ken Burnett for bringing this about!

Three things stand out for us:

1. The individuals or families that you connected from the congregation to particular brothers and/or sisters in the UK was a source of joy to those in need here. They first of all appreciated hearing *personally* from the MMT contacts. Most of the recipients of this grace were Russian speakers who did not know English. There was only one exception. So, I (Howard) would get a call from different ones to help them understand in Hebrew what had been written, and to help them write something back in English. This also blessed me to see the openness of each one on both sides to share aspects of their lives and their prayer requests. When financial support also began to come in (almost from the beginning), that was a total surprise to them, and they were very appreciative. For some of them, this extra bonus provided temporary relief to the small incomes or pensions that they may have had.

2. One dear, older couple here would often send a sizeable jar of local _honey_ in the mail back to their "partners" and benefactors. I remember that this actually caused some anxiety on the other side, partly because it became a *lot* of honey over time, and also because it was not quite legal to import honey into the UK. Not to mention, what would it have been like had the containers leaked

for some reason. Despite asking this dear couple to not send any more honey, and that the recipients were very thankful for what had already been received, this dear couple continued to send more until a "yellow card" was waved. God bless them!

3. At some point you took an interest in also reaching out to Israeli Arab believers. That was so good and right, and a further expression of what the Holy Spirit would do through MMT to demonstrate that our Father loves all of His children and knows each of their situations. We all need to love and know that we are loved; and that is what you did by expanding the ministry of grace and comfort to our brothers and sisters who often felt/feel dismissed.

God bless you two, Kathy and Tony, for having such a large giving heart, and for faithfully carrying out what you had received from the Lord Jesus Christ to do for Him and for His brethren in need here in Israel, and in Nachalat Yeshua in particular. Your love and friendship have been precious through the years, and we always enjoy being in your company. Even as MMT learned to adapt to some changing realities, you continued to press on showing that what you had received from the Lord was dependent mostly upon Him to sustain. And He has! Someday, not that far off, we will see a lot more of you in a far better world that our God and Saviour will create!

Eric Benson, Director House of Victory, Haifa

In the year 2006, as I reviewed the financial situation of House of Victory, I realized we were falling into a desperate situation which I needed to report to Pastor David Davis. It seemed the most responsible choice would be to lay off one of our staff workers. When I told this to Pastor David, he said, "There may be a way to get help." He wrote a letter to a ministry in England called the Mount Moriah Trust, led by Tony and Kathy Stewart asking if it would be possible to help with a contribution to staff member Grisha's salary. They agreed and so through a series of perfectly timed events Grisha was able, with their help and support, to continue to work at House of Victory. We did not have to lay him off. That was an absolute miracle.

When they visited Israel later that year, David introduced me to Tony and Kathy. Immediately, there was a sense that there was something special about this couple as they shared with me their passion and vision for the Trust. They made a long term commitment to stand together and support this precious brother. Over the next decade the Mount Moriah Trust stood alongside Grisha and his wife and children with financial support that enabled them to pay their bills and put food on the table. I have such great memories over the years of observing how Tony and Kathy truly came up alongside this brother. Because there was a communication problem, I needed to always arrange a translator for their meetings. Usually Tony and Kathy would try to make a commitment to meet with Grisha once a year, whenever they were visiting the land of Israel from England. I remember those times together when Tony and Kathy would come and sit at the dining table of House of Victory. Then they would go and sit privately in the corner with Gregory and the translator. These were times of great fellowship, laughter and prayer, and even tears together. As time went on, Tony and his wife would go directly to Grisha's house and have dinner with his wife and children. When Grisha later had to stop working at House of Victory, because he was sick with hepatitis and undergoing treatment, the Trust faithfully continued their support, which was a great help to him and his family during that difficult time.

Later, Grisha got a vision to start a private business of woodworking design and a gift shop. A Mount Moriah Trust supporter's heart was touched by the Lord to provide the funds to buy all the equipment that was necessary. This was a beautiful expression of Christian love for a brother. Grisha says that he and his family are very thankful for God's great help and support and the way that He brought Tony and Kathy into their lives.

Over the years, Tony and Kathy also saw the work of House of Victory, and the Lord put it on their hearts to come up alongside our ministry. The Trust began to support us on a regular basis. Such a blessing it is to have had the opportunity to witness the growth, the development and the anointing of this beautiful work. It has been my privilege and honour to develop a close friendship with this precious couple. We have first-hand witnessed the tremendous fruit of their ministry. Even as Mount Moriah is known as a place of sacrifice, Tony and Kathy gave their lives in service and continue to be a poured out drink offering on behalf of the needy here in the land of Israel.

The Word of God tells us in Eph. 5:2, "And walk in love as Messiah also has loved us and given Himself for us, an offering and a sacrifice to God for a sweet-smelling aroma." Paul is writing to us how as followers of God we need to imitate His love. I can testify that the Mount Moriah Trust and Tony and Kathy are a sacrificial offering of great love with a sweet-smelling aroma.

Eric Benson
Director
House of Victory

Pastor Tal & Tigi Shiferaw, Kehilat Beit El, Jerusalem

First, Mount Moriah Trust is the Number One faithful partner for our church. We met you when the Church of Bethel was founded. Personally, you have been a father and mother to our family and our children. You have helped us in our times of need. You have helped us with our debts, helped our children and helped us to feed our family.

In our congregation the Trust has enabled us to help those who are sick and those who are hungry. Beyond that, you are our family and in your spiritual lives you have demonstrated Jesus' life in many ways. You have given us your time and have shared teaching with our congregation and have shared much spiritual fellowship with us. You have visited many of our church members in their homes blessing them with prayer. Thank you.

Steve Dunham, Healing and Discipleship Ministry

I have known of the work of Mount Moriah Trust since I first met Tony and Kathy at Ellel Ministries Pierrepont, near Farnham in Surrey nearly fifteen years ago. I was impressed by their sincerity to help the poor and needy in Israel. They prayerfully seek donations from Christians to support needy Believers in Israel and share of their ministry at church groups in numerous countries around the world and the UK. MMT is a unique ministry in that not only does it help people from all communities in Israel, but they do not take out any administration costs from the donations they receive for Believers in Israel. These costs are covered another way.

I look forward to each visit Tony and Kathy make to Israel, to be encouraged and share good fellowship with them. They know many leaders in the Land and are able to help needy people by giving money via the local leadership specific to the project or person in need. This is evaluated each year and either stopped or continued. This accountability is a mark of the integrity of their charity. I strongly encourage anyone to support this ministry.

Pastor Efraim & Jeannie Goldstein, Kehilat Or HaGalil, Nahariyya

Western Galilee is a very diverse community in Israel. The population is divided between Jews, Arabs, Druze and other groups which include a large population of Lebanese people. The Congregation that I was called to pastor, Kehila Or Hagalil (Light of Galilee) is a small congregation founded in 1976 by two immigrants from England, Ruth and Albert Nessim.

This unique missionary couple established a Congregation built on Jews, Arabs, Lebanese and other people from eight different countries. When I came up to Nahariyya to serve this diverse and unique Congregation there were challenges that we face.

In the Congregation was a couple, Pierre and Maggie Altounian who fled southern Lebanon with their three children in the year 2000. After arriving in Israel, Pierre who had been an officer in the Southern Lebanese Army came to true faith in Jesus. He had a deep desire to share his newfound faith with others in the Lebanese community. He was well known among many of the former Lebanese Army soldiers. His native tongue was Arabic and he also loved sharing the Gospel with both Christians and Moslem.

I realized that partnering with Pierre would be the way the Lord was leading to open up avenues of better evangelism amongst the Arab Christians and the Lebanese community in Northern Israel. The challenge is Pierre works a full time job and has five children at home.

My prayer for our ministry at Kehila Or Hagalil was that we could raise financial support for Pierre. With some assistance he would have more time to reach out to the Arab and Lebanese communities.

It was just at that same time, my wife and I were visiting England. We were participating in a Church celebration and were introduced to Tony and Kathy. We were so blessed when they agreed to provide funds to help Pierre and his ministry. The Or Galalil Congregation is greatly encouraged by God's support through the Mount Moriah Trust.

Pastor Zechariah & Alemaz Arni, Retzon Ha'El congregation, Haifa

Retzon Ha'El congregation here in Haifa, Israel is thankful for your love and faithfulness through the years. For us MMT is part of our kingdom work and you have influenced a lot in the ministry that we are doing here. I see your love I see your heart to the kingdom and you do all this with humbleness.

I would say that I know many organisations, but you are not just part of the things that we are doing, you also part of our family. I believe that people who support MMT can be happy because you are so trustful. To be honest I don't have enough words to express your love for us, but I know one thing that our God will reward you.

We love you and are thankful for all the people who support MMT. May the God of Israel bless you.

Anis & Nawal Barhoum – House of Light in Shefar Am

We would like to share with you these testimonies:

Seeing a lump in his throat, and tears welling up in the eyes of "F" we understood the great need for a divine solution for his problem. Besides being in prison he was hurting double portion because of the suffering of his sweet wife and children. He needed to believe that the Lord still loves him and is waiting for him to confess his sin and repent. Accepting the Lord Jesus into his life brought light and joy inside him and he asked us to visit his family. He wanted them to know Jesus as he has done, then and only then they can forgive him and accept him in his home again once he's finished his confinement.

We walked into the tiny simple family home, with Tony & Kathy a very special anointed couple who are prayer warriors and supporters for people in such situations. We have known them for many years already as co-workers (co supporters) in The Body of Christ in Israel. The Lord went before us and prepared the ground and as we came in we felt His presence in us and in the place.

Colossians 3: 12: *Put on therefore, as God's elect, holy and beloved, a heart of compassion, kindness, lowliness, meekness, longsuffering;*

Our hearts went towards the family. Tony and Kathy prayed with each and every one there. We could tell the house needed some renovation and some furniture. But that's too much money. They agreed with us that this family is in great need. They already support House of Light as they do with many congregations, churches and ministries. With this in mind the Lord showed us some volunteers to do the work in stages and along the year. We bought paint one month, paid electricity bill another month, paid school fees the third month, renovated the broken bathroom, etc..

With the support of "Mount Moriah Trust" and the praying partners we could see the big difference in the attitude and behaviour of the family members. Their hearts were filled with the Lord's love. Forgiveness took over and when the father came out of prison he was accepted with deep love and willingness to give him his place as the head of their family, all being submissive to this "New Head" who is filled with Jesus ideas and discipline.

The whole family is walking with the Lord in steadfast steps now for some good years. They even help counsel other families who are passing through difficult experiences and trials

Don't return now to the yesterdays.
Let go of all the burning care,
There is a greater joy found in the pain.
It is a burden for ME to bear (Jesus)

The encouraging thing about Tony & Kathy is the trust that they put in the ministries they support. They give us freedom to decide who to help with their support. This gives us peace and joy doing the thing with relief.

One family we have been supporting for quite few years through the Mount Moriah gifts, is a single parent "N" with three children. She had her ups and downs all through the years yet the Love of Jesus would bring her back to HIM each time stronger than before. Her children's school trips were paid, clothing was cared for, sent to swimming courses and needed books were always with them as they went into the classroom. She joined a discipleship training course then inner healing sessions together with other participants, all supported by the MMT. "N" could always buy meat and cook good food for her children as she also got dry food from House of Light.

Nowadays this family still has difficulties, but we can tell the difference, the renewal and commitment for the Lord that this mother made. Positive thinking is ruling her life and the joy of the Lord is her strength Mount Moriah Trust and House of Light pushing the cart together saved this woman from being thrown in the streets, committing suicide or lost in a bad choice. She knows for sure that Jesus never left nor forsaken her, and she knows that the One who saved her will surely help her children to accept Him someday soon. Trusting His sovereignty and almighty power, she keeps lifting them in her prayers before the throne.

I will be Your peace, Trust Me, I will be Your light.
Rest now, I fought for your purity.
In Me there is no night.
Let Me pick up all the pieces of your life
scattered o'er the floor,
Then lift your face up to My love,
and you will see the open door.

Tony & Kathy are people chosen to have many, many children. They do their work perfectly. All year round, they keep in touch with congregations, churches and ministries they support and once a year they would fly into Israel, go with them to visit and encourage families they hold in their hearts. It meant and still means a lot to each family to see their supporters and care takers face to face. By that, the families feel they are not just numbers nor items. They are loved, chosen and adopted by Jesus who shows HIS love to them through this unique couple and all those who stand behind them. Families would even phone and ask us about when Tony and Kathy are coming. "We miss them. They are our real parents" they say, proudly and with great honour!!

The feeling of belonging to the big Mount Moriah Trust family, is so important to these needy families who have lost much of their trust in themselves and their abilities to live with their heads uplifted. They also lack trust in people around, who are not giving them their true value as humans but deal with them as losers or a "well with no bottom". The minute they feel the real embracing family, they just cannot help but drop some tears of "overwhelming joy". They say: "There are still good people in this world who know we are alive! Who really care for our success! Who give us a hand out of the miry clay."

"S" is one of the many families MMT cares for. Wife of an alcoholic who abuses verbally and physically. Mother of three who suffered and suffered with no glimpse of light and hope. By MMT's support their daughter was able to complete her studies at a Bible College. Their electricity bill was always paid and the family members gained their position amongst people in the wide family and in town. One of the sons and also the daughter got married and formed healthy families with three children each. Though the parents are very sick physically, still the wife blesses the Lord who gave her counsel and even at the darkest times her heart instructs her.

We at House of Light do not find words that can thank you enough for answering the Lord's calling upon your lives. For accepting the difficult mission of being parents of so many, caring to teach them to believe in themselves and that the happiest of people don't necessarily have the best of everything; They just make the most of everything.

Pastor Ariel & Keren Revach, Calling of Israel congregation, Ramla

In 2007 when we moved from the city of Ashdod to Ramla to start a new congregation, as there was not a single messianic congregation in this city.

At that time the city of Ramla and the neighbouring city of Lod were some of the most criminal cities in Israel and the centre of the drug trade. Many people with a low standard of living lived there – single mothers, new immigrants, Holocaust Survivors.

We were thinking of starting work with drug addicts, but the Lord directed us to work with people in need. We started working with a small group of believers, many single mums and pensioners came to congregation. Today single mums and pensioners make up 70 percent of the congregation.

In 2013, I met Tony and Kathy Stewart from the ministry of Mount Moriah. They arrived in Ramla and visited several families and single mothers. Their heart was touched to financially support these families and also me and my family.

We are very grateful to the ministry of Mount Moriah for their open hearts, their support and their participation in the life of the congregation and my family.

Pastor Dima & Elmira Brodkin – Grace House Church & Ministries in Beer Sheba

Our family of five came to Israel twenty years ago (May 13, 1999). Two adults and three children and five bags of things are all that we were allowed to take with us according to the norms and number of people leaving. When we arrived in Israel we had no money and no means to rent a house. The help from the State that we received in Ben Gurion was 1000 shekels for the whole family.

Therefore, Elmira and I started looking for work from the first days. There was no talk of ulpans. We needed not only an apartment, but also all things and basic necessities. In August 1999, we accidentally found a Community in Be'er Sheva. Since arriving we did not have any contacts or addresses of the Community, and it was really a miracle when in the old city we saw the sign of the Bible House store.

From that moment, the acquaintance with the Messianic community began. In 2002, we as a family began to receive financial and prayer help from the MMT, and this was and still remains a huge support and blessing not only for our family, but also for many families and individuals in our community, we are very grateful to the Lord for your love, support and prayers for His people in the Holy Land. We pray for you and your ministry and all the people who participate in this work.

Christine Sakakibara, Narkis Street Baptist Church

Rachel T has been one of those who has been greatly helped by MMT. She first came to Jerusalem in 1981 and God stirred her heart to find a way to help Israel in a practical way. She was not Jewish but still was able to move to Jerusalem to serve as a nurse in Hadassah hospital in 1985. She was a nurse in the Neurological department and it tested her on every level. She had to learn medical terms in Hebrew and endure long shifts with critically ill patients. However, working under this kind of intense pressure, gave her an opportunity to openly speak of her faith to many family members and patients. She remembers those years as the most spiritually rewarding of her life.

Sadly, over time the pressure to pull long shifts together with physical and mental weariness began to take its toll on her. She experienced burn out on a scale she had never known and eventually had a breakdown, leaving her unable to return to her nursing career. The death of her parents in England also added to her emotional collapse and soon she found herself unable to make the smallest decisions or manage her life on her small income. Eventually she became homeless in Jerusalem, her only companion a devoted dog, and moved around from place to place with a few suitcases. While living this kind of life she came in touch with others who were "down on their luck" and spontaneously began a street ministry, encouraging them spiritually and sharing the little she had. She epitomized the description of a generous woman given in Proverbs 31:20 "She opens her hand to the poor and reaches out her hands to the needy".

Rachel today, is still in Jerusalem, and still reaching out to those society judges and questions. She has no permanent home but enjoys the generosity and companionship of precious saints of God who open their hearts and homes to her as the spirit of God touches them. She house sits, dog sits and now has a small pension from the UK to keep her off the streets. Without the help of MMT she would have had to make the street her permanent home.

Pastor Munir & Sharon Kakish, Home of New Life, Ramallah

Since 2012 we at RCO Ministries in the Holy Land (Home of New Life) have partnered with Mount Moriah Trust. We so much appreciate Brother Tony and Sister Kathy. They are a living example of what it means to be a disciple! I love their integrity.

For many years, Mt. Moriah has sponsored children in our children's ministries here in Ramallah and the West Bank, even helping a family in Gaza through us! Many of the children we help have come from horrible backgrounds and are way behind in their studies. One of these was a child named Jeries. With the prayers and support of sponsors we were able to help save Jeries' life! We worked with him. Eventually he finished high school and was accepted into college. A few years later at his engagement he related how much he was indebted to the Home for helping him. Thank you for helping us to save young Christian boys such as Jeries who now works at the American Embassy in Jerusalem. Quite a feat for a poor village boy!

Mt. Moriah has also helped support young girls who come from needy, fragile families. We are so glad for Mt. Moriah's help. We so much appreciate Brother Tony and Sister Kathy, especially for coming to the children's home and interacting with the kids. Mt. Moriah has been a faithful partner in ministering to the children. God bless all of you for your ministry.

Pastor Yossi & Ronit Ovadia, Kekilat Haderech, Karmiel

Karmiel being a peripheral city that has a large number of new immigrants, struggling to settle in the new country, and a large number of low income population, amongst them families of single moms, we as a congregation had put it in our priority to help and put special efforts towards helping these people get established financially and spiritually as healthy families and individuals.

Along the years we came across many funds and organizations that purposed their goal to help this population with Humanitarian Aid (food bags, rent, etc...) which were extremely necessary and basic for first crisis situation. But the challenges of settling in a new country with new language and often the need to be retrained in a profession or finding a new profession, means that it takes several years for a family to struggle through with a very low income.

But then after this initial period of time the families get to the "gray" daily routine of daily struggles and frustrations. Seeing their children struggling burdens them all. Praying for stability, and for their children to settle and stay away from the streets and loss of focus and identity. There is where The Mount Moriah fund help came in so timely. As Kathy and Tony introduced themselves asking us "how can we help?" we asked them to fill in this special niche that though it does not seem a "basic need" was so needed! So, since 2013 the Mount Moriah Fund help us to help these families by:

- Helping kids complete their education (helping pay high school fees).
- Adding an after school education (music and sports) to help the children stay out of the streets, and help them find their personal abilities and strength.
- Helping with extracurricular lesson for children with special needs (basic lessons or other special add help).
- Giving these families help to buy the school supplies at the beginning of school year and at times even to buy school clothes.

On top of this we were able to direct help to support the Messianic summer activities for the children of the congregation. Whether going out to Messianic Israelis summer camps or making it possible for us as a congregation to make our own summer camp.

All in all, we were so blessed with this faithful support and getting to know Tony and Kathy in person. We have added personal testimonies from some of the people that were blessed that you may too be blessed.

Alona and Sasha Kravich

Thank you very much for your financial support that helps us pay for music lessons for our son Andrey. Doctors diagnosed him with autism. Music lessons were recommended by a specialist who works with him. Classical music has a positive effect on the functioning of the brain, and playing the piano develops motor skills. Because of your financial support we were able to find a music teacher who works with autistic children. These lessons helped our son to develop some skills and he became interested in music. Without your help, it would be very difficult for us to pay for these lessons because we also pay for other classes.

Thank you for your help! Be blessed!

Shelly Alimi

My name is Shelly Alimi a single mother of two sons Daniel and Eyal. We live in Karmiel, North of Israel. Few years ago (2014) My son Daniel started playing basketball, after a short period of time I realised that I couldn't pay for it. I contacted our congregation "Kehilat Haderech" for financial help The help we received was beyond financial, Daniel played on the basketball team, he developed social skills and friends. Next month Daniel is celebrating his 21st Birthday. Today he is serving in the Israel Defense Forces and to this day he is playing basketball almost every day. I want to thank God and your organization for their help and support. I pray that God will continue to bless you so that you can give more help to other families. Blessing in the name of Yeshua.

Gilad Inbar and Dvir Bousi

We are an Israeli family, with three children. Our oldest son, Dvir (now sixteen), started to learn guitar when he was nine years old with a group of children as an activity that was provided by another congregation. After two lessons his teacher called us to say that Dvir had a special talent and a quick perception, and that we should help him developing his talent. In that group of children, he couldn't really progress, so we decide to take private lessons with the same teacher. The cost was not too high and we were able to pay for them.

After one year, the teacher said to us that he couldn't move forward with our son because he (the teacher) got to his maximum level of teaching with Dvir, and he didn't want to waste his time. So, he recommended us to send him to an official music school, where he could really progress and grow, since he was growing fast into the "world of music" and it became a huge part of him.

After finding out what was the tuition fee for that music school, we realized we could never afford it. We shared our situation with Pastor Yossi Ovadia, who decided to send our request to you. We praise the Lord for your support. Dvir was able to study at the music school for two years, and those studies indeed contributed to his professional level. He started on the classic guitar and after one year he started to learn on the electric guitar.

The music and the guitar became a huge part of his life, and every day that passes, he becomes more and more of a musician. Not only his playing is getting better but also his ability to improvise and compose music. Now Dvir is an essential part of our congregation's worship team. He is now starting his preparations to his final exam on music that will take place in two years.

All of that would not have been possible without your support, and MMT has played a big part in making our son who he is today. We praise the Lord for you and for the project that you started, and for your heart and willingness to give.

The generous man will be prosperous, and he who waters will himself be watered. Proverbs 11:25

GO TO THE LAND OF MORIAH

Emil Briginski

My name is Emil Briginski and I'm twenty-one years old. I'm now serving in the army and about to finish my service in two months. I want to thank you for your donations, which have enabled me to learn the guitar professionally.

I began to learn playing the guitar nine years ago; I had been studying with a private teacher who is also a believer. After a while I decided to stop, because I thought that I had reached the level I wanted. Then I joined the worship team, and started to learn in a guitar class in the congregation, with a different teacher. The teacher recommended me to go and learn how to play professionally in a music school, and after I talk with Yossi and Gilad I started to learn there. I'm giving thanks to the Lord for you and your help that allow me to study at the music school.

After my first lesson at the music school with my new teacher, he recommends me to start taking theory lessons on music, to help me understand better what I'm playing and hearing. After three years at the music school, and a few exams I feel that I have been equipped with a lot of tools and I am feeling more comfortable and secure with my playing. Thank you so much for your financial support, it was a big blessing to me and to my life.

Pastor Hani Billan, Cana Baptist Church, Kfar Cana

At the beginning of my ministry, I was invited to the UK to participate in a prayer conference for Israel and to visit some of the churches over there. During one of the services in the conference, I was asked to talk about my ministry, and so I stood up and spoke all that was on my heart and I spoke about all the challenges we face with our ministry. At the end, all the brothers and sisters over there were given the opportunity to ask about our ministry, it was amazing, and they are all just very kind.

A year had passed after my visit, and I got a call from Tony and Kathy from the UK, and I had not met them personally, or even remember having seen them before. But they were at the conference I previously mentioned. And they had also heard me speaking about our ministry and all the challenges we face, and the Lord touched their heart and they were so interested in our ministry and the work we do. So, they called, and they told us about their intentions to help and support three families in our church that are in need. So, they would send each family 750 NIS (which is about 100 pounds back then), every three months. And that is how our relationship with the Mount Moriah Service began.

A year or two later, they started supporting five families, in addition to me and another brother who serves at our church. Their support has always been a great blessing to us and to our ministry for it always comes on time and is the reason for great blessings for the families in need.

I remember one situation that touched my heart, when I went to deliver the money to one of the families, I gave it to the husband and I was surprised when he told me: "I thank the Lord for His goodness, up until this morning I couldn't afford to buy milk for my children, and I was looking all over the house for money, and now the Lord is giving me more than double the amount I need, praise the Lord".

During the summer, we hold a vacation bible school (summer camp) at our church. 120-150 kids participate in this camp every year, and so many of these kids' families cannot afford to pay the camp fees which are 250 NIS for each kid, especially when they enroll more than one child. So, the church exempts them from paying, while the Mount Moriah Trust contribution makes up for that money for these children. They are a reason for the joy of many kids.

Your spiritual support to us in prayer is one of the things that keeps us going. We are also thankful for our sister Kathy who takes part in the women's service and who has always been a great blessing and encouragement for them.

On behalf of me, and all your brothers and sisters in the Cana Baptist Church, thank you for all that you have done, and still are doing for our ministry. You are such a great blessing for us and for God's work in our Land.

Pastor Israel Pochtar, Beit Hallel Ashdod Testimonies

Ksenia's Testimony

Ksenia is a young mother who came to Israel with her husband and three children from Vladivostok one year ago. Our follow-up team came into contact with Ksenia and her family through family members of theirs who were attending Beit Hallel. They were facing a hard time adapting to life in Israel and needed help desperately, as juggling Hebrew, work, and family life was proving to be draining and overwhelming. Upon our team's invitation, they started visiting Beit Hallel and attending our family and alpha courses.

When they gave their hearts to Jesus they blossomed and started getting very much involved with volunteering and helping at Beit Hallel. We became aware that Ksenia and her family's financial situation had not improved and that they were being strained to make ends meet. We informed them that our feeding project was also meant for them, because the Lord had instructed us to find every need everywhere and to fill it. We signed them up for our feeding project and they started receiving regular aid in the form of monthly food hampers, clothing and appliances from Beit Hallel.

Ksenia was shocked to hear that our food hampers were

being supplied through the support of Christians throughout the world. She wept tears of joy as she realised that her perception of Christians had been wrong, and that the Jewish people have multitudes of Christians who love and support them.

Organisations like Mount Moriah Trust are bringing change to Israeli society by transforming the lives of believers in need through feeding and clothing them. Our work at Beit Hallel is crucial for many Israeli families at Beit Hallel Congregation, and that's why we rely so heavily on the support and love of organisations such as the Mount Moriah Trust.

Anna's Testimony

Anna, her husband and two children were living in Lugansk, Ukraine. They both had a good solid job, had their own home, children were happy, they were surrounded by family and friends and their life was good.

That's when political disruptions started taking place in Ukraine, and things quickly escalated to full blown war shortly after. They were living under constant fire, and Anna decided to take her children and flee to her sister that lived farther away. Her husband stayed behind so that their house wasn't left unattended.

Months have passed and Anna was missing her home and husband, she was dreaming about coming back. She felt she didn't care how bad the situation was, if she had her family with her, all would be well. That if there was no running water, she would go to the river to get water. If there was no gas, she would make fire to cook. But things weren't exactly as she imagined.

Anna came back home to Lugansk, and realised there was no food for her family. They were living now in a war zone, salaries haven't been paid in nine months, there was only grain and beans that was distributed to people, and even then it was so little that people fought in line to get some for their families.

Then she found out there was a Jewish organisation helping with food packets once a month. Her kids were devouring the products she was able to receive once a month, but even the supposed monthly help was oftentimes irregular and wouldn't come. Anna was desperate and didn't know what to do, when she heard from a friend there about "Eben Ezer" organization that was helping Jews come to Israel. She started preparing all their documents to make Aliyah to Israel. They arrived in Ashdod with no money, no belongings, with the little they were able to bring with them. It was a very difficult season for them, but then someone testified to Anna how she had found hope and friends at Beit Hallel Congregation.

They started to attend our services and slotted into a home-group. Anna eventually gave her life to Jesus and felt a peace that she could never have imagined. Her husband and kids saw the change in her life, which led to her husband giving his life to Jesus. In the meantime, Anna and her family's financial situation grew worse to the point where she applied to our humanitarian projects department for help.

Due to the help of our donors and friends like the Mount Moriah Trust, we were able to put her family on the list of families that receive humanitarian help from us on a monthly basis. Every month Anna receives a food hamper from Beit Hallel, which contains nutritious and non-perishable food items. We were also able to bless her children with school supplies, clothing, as well as other day-to-day necessities.

She testified that she was so touched by the care and attention she received here with us, which aside from the monthly food packets, were a breath of fresh air for her and her family.

Arthur and Mary's Testimony

Arthur Makarov, his wife Mary, and their three young children have quite a story to share! They are Jewish immigrants to the land of Israel who had fled the Ukraine in the hope of finding a better life for them and their children. Jews in the Ukraine face a tremendous amount of discrimination and hardship in the form of anti-Semitism and hate crimes, in addition to the struggle that daily life has become due to the civil war raging in the Ukraine. Since Mary was a doctor in the Ukraine, they had to come and live in Ashdod's absorption centre for new immigrant doctors. The first three years are always very tough for these dear ones, as they have to start from scratch and build their lives anew.

Arthur and Mary eventually found Beit Hallel Congregation through the testimony of close friends at the absorption centre. They started attending our services and gave their lives to Jesus, after which their lives changed radically. They were on fire for Jesus and the Lord had rekindled a fresh new hope in their hearts and they knew that their new lives in Israel would be blessed.

While Arthur and Mary were integrating into Israeli society, they also had to study Hebrew and work, which led to severe financial challenges and the inability to always put sufficient amounts of food on the table. They applied to our feeding project and started getting monthly food hampers, children's care hampers and clothing from Beit Hallel. They testify that our help played a massive role in allowing themselves to be established as Israelis who can stand on their own two feet.

Our partners and friends like the Mount Moriah Trust have had a tremendous impact on the lives of new Jewish immigrants like Arthur and Mary, through their generosity, prayers and love. Arthur and Mary's story is a stirring account of facing overwhelming odds, but finding support, love and compassion through the aid of our partners and friends like the Mount Moriah Trust.

Pastor Tony Sperandeo, Kehilat HaMaayan, Kfar Saba

Mount Moriah Trust is helping us to meet the material needs of our growing congregation. New immigrants arrive with almost nothing from Ukraine, Africa, India – all different parts of the world. The congregation is not only their spiritual home but also provides for their basic needs that the Israeli government is not providing at this moment. When Mount Moriah came to us it was the right place at the right time! They provide assistance with very specific needs in the lives of individuals, especially single mothers who have a difficult time to make a living. Social security in Israel is quite low as far as income is concerned, so we are trying to help them build a budget and through that be able to pay the rent, school books for the children and their other basic needs. We distribute food coupons for the supermarket and food parcels and MMT has really been helping us with those. If we did not have that support, we would have to go back to the Lord and cry: "Lord send other donors!"

I believe that the Lord has a heart for the poor and needy and He will never leave them without provision. He has chosen the Mount Moriah Trust to provide for them.

Chapter 28

Supporters' Testimonies

For we are co-workers in God's service; you are God's field,
God's building. 1 Corinthians 3:9

In this chapter I have included just a few testimonies from supporters with the intention of demonstrating how God touches people's hearts to support the work.

Pastor John Angliss had only known Tony and I for a short time but he encouraged us from the outset and agreed to bring his Godly wisdom to the work by joining the very first Board of Trustees. In his testimony Pastor John mentions visits to pastors in Israel whilst leading tours. Visiting the "Living Stones" is something that we have always very much encouraged whenever we speak. Over the years we have arranged and facilitated many groups to meet Jewish and Arab pastors either by going to their churches or by having the pastors visit the tour group in their hotel.

Sally Williams first met us in Jerusalem with a friend, Rosie who was meeting her adopted prayer partner. As you will read, this personal relationship was immediately attractive to her. Sally now serves on the Board of Trustees, but more than that she makes personal visits to the pastors and congregations on behalf of the Trust which is most helpful as it takes some weight off our shoulders in maintaining relationships. We are so thankful that Mark Dunman, also a trustee, and his wife Margaret have also been able to do this as you will have read in Chapter 13. We have been so blessed that both Sally and Mark have covered their own travel and accommodation expenses whilst doing this.

Tony and Sally Tester and Brian and Brenda Baldwin are long term supporters of the work who have valued the connections that the Trust has provided with believers in God's Land.

I have included two testimonies from supporters in Singapore. We were put in touch with Nethanel and Tabitha Lam by Christine Sakakibara of Narkis Street Baptist Church in Jerusalem. In advance of our arrival they had arranged some meetings for us but we only met for the first time at the meeting which took place in the Bible House. Gwenda Kuo was also at this meeting. God sowed the first seeds for the Trust in Singapore that evening and in the days that followed. We have been blessed to have their support and friendship ever since.

Finally, we have a short message from Wayne and Pauline Perry whom we first met in Ballina on the coast of NSW, Australia. Meeting them was another divine connection; the Lord put together people who loved and prayed for Israel and the Jewish people, with the Trust who could provide a practical means for them to bless Israel. Wayne and Pauline have recently taken over the mantle of MMT representatives in Australia.

Shalom Israel has become the Trust's largest and most important partner in Australia. You will have read Shalom Israel's co-founder Pat Ramsay's testimony in Chapter 21.

The Trust provides spiritual as well as financial support to the believers. Each month we issue a Prayer Letter which provides:

- News and Prayer points for Israel and its relationship with its neighbours.
- News and Prayer points for the Messianic Fellowships and Christian Arab Churches.

For many prayer partners this information has transformed their prayers from generalisations to focused prayers dealing with specific current issues that are important for the country and the pastors and congregations. We put this information together from a wide range of newsletters and communications originating in Israel, Gaza and the West Bank. We are not claiming the Trust to be unique in doing this, there are several other organizations that do similar things.

If you would like to receive this information you can *subscribe* by visiting our website: mountmoriah.org.uk

Testimonies

Pastor John Angliss, Ark Christian Fellowship and Ambassador International Ministry (AIM), UK

It is with great pleasure and thanks to God that I am able to write a contribution to this book about the Mount Moriah Trust. I have known Tony and Kathy for a number of years and they were for some of that time attendees and members at South of Reading Christian Fellowship (SORCF) which I led for forty years from 1977 to 2017. This fellowship was known for its support and prayer for Israel and the Jewish people and God's purposes in the Bible concerning them. For my own part, I and then the Church were supporters of Prayer for Israel and Derek Prince ministries both of which I was a trustee for a number of years.

Therefore, it was no great surprise when Tony and Kathy joined us and even more encouraging when they received a vision to help needy Messianic Jews and Christian Arabs in Israel. For the Church, this enhanced the already existing vision and prayer described. In 2002, they formed the Mount Moriah Trust and I was privileged to be one of the original five trustees and with Ken Burnett, founder of Prayer of Israel, as the Patron.

On Sunday, 20th May 2007, we laid hands on Tony and Kathy at a special commissioning service to release them to take the ministry of MMT to a wider audience. I well remember this morning service. At the last minute I was led by the Holy Spirit to change my prepared message, I quickly popped out into the Church office and with a quick prayer changed it to a study of the Biblical Mount Moriah as first described in Genesis 22.

This outline of this message can be found in Chapter 5. It is a witness to the Lord's confirmation of His purposes for Tony and Kathy and the ongoing progress and fruitfulness of MMT. Sometime later, Tony & Kathy were led to worship at a Fellowship a little closer to where they lived, but the SORCF support of MMT continued and has done until this day. I retired as a trustee on 17th April 2013, only through time constraints and continue to follow with prayerful interest and support the trust's work.

From small beginnings, it has grown immensely as this book will reveal and now has international support as well. On more than one occasion, when I have been either leading or teaching on tours to Israel, Tony and Kathy have met up with our group at a hotel to meet the people and share about their work. Unlike many ministries, they personally visit the places and people which the Trust supports, and it is to their credit and perhaps a lesson to others, that they never do any of this for personal profit or gain, all their expenses are covered privately.

It is also a testimony to the Lord that whilst believing in God's purposes for Israel as clearly revealed in the Scriptures, many Christian Arabs have benefitted from the Trust and I have had the privilege of meeting one or two of these.

Like Jabez of old, the Lord has *enlarged their coast* (1 Chronicles 4:10) and only eternity will reveal how many have been blessed, encouraged and perhaps even survived by the Spirit led giving of MMT. Matthew 25:40 comes to mind in that great parable of the Sheep and the Goats, which of course has clear application to Israel, *"Inasmuch as you have done it unto one of the least of these MY BRETHREN, you have done it unto me".* [emphasis added].

With many others, we rejoice in the goodness of the Lord thus displayed to date, and pray that this work will go on from strength to strength, that its founders will be led, guided, strengthened, and directed by the Holy Spirit and given much wisdom in the disbursement of help to needy believers in the land. I commend this ministry to you. Praise and honour to the Lord for all that has been accomplished and in anticipation of what will be done before the Lord returns.

Sally Williams – Mount Moriah Trustee

It was in the beautiful old foyer of the Dan Panorama Hotel, Jerusalem, that I first met Kathy and Tony in 2007. I was in Israel for a week with a group of Christians who I had travelled with before, but this time I had invited a good friend of mine, Rosie, to come along too, and we were going to stay on an extra few days to visit some more of the land and also to learn more about some Christian charities working in Israel. One evening Rosie asked whether I would be interested in seeing a lady she supported through the Mount Moriah Trust, a charity I had not heard of before. I was intrigued. What had impressed me so much, was that Rosie was going to actually meet someone who she had been able to help by funding much-needed dental work. It is rare that those who give to charities actually see the people they are supporting, and I was almost as excited as Rosie!

It was a delightful evening and meeting the lovely lady whose teeth had been saved by Rosie's financial gift was quite emotional. She was so grateful, and Rosie was so pleased to be able to sit and chat with her and learn more about her.

We were joined by Kathy and Tony Stewart who were

visiting Israel in connection with their charity, the Mount Moriah Trust. It was through them that Rosie had come to know Esther and I found it fascinating to hear all about the work with which they were involved. I knew straight away that there was something very unique about the charity, and it did not take long to realise that the difference was the 'personal touch'. This was not a charity whose officers were working remotely from those they were supporting; this was a charity whose very ethic was to come alongside, quite literally, the very people they felt called by God to provide for not only financially, but also spiritually, through prayer and relationship. As I talked with Kathy and Tony, and heard about the work of the charity and the groups of people they assisted in so many different ways according to their specific needs, I felt that this was a work which was so very much in line with the teaching of Scripture; to provide for those of our brothers and sisters in the family of God who are burdened or in need.

Taking my leave of Kathy and Tony that evening, I gave them my contact details and they sent me regular newsletters from the charity. We stayed in contact and they would give me regular news updates concerning the growing number of congregations throughout Israel supported by the Mount Moriah Trust. It was in one of these newsletters, some while after that first meeting, that I read an article about a church in Cana whose Pastor commented that it saddened him that so many Christian tourists came to Israel to look at the old stones, but very few came to see the 'living stones', the present day Christians in the land who sometimes are very much on the front line. That phrase about the 'living stones' feeling that Christians visiting Israel were only interested in sightseeing really affected me, and I contacted Kathy and Tony to see if it would be possible for me to meet any of the Pastors whose congregations the Trust supported. I felt very privileged that they gave me their permission to do so, and over the years since I am extremely humbled to be able to count some of these Pastors and their wives as dear friends.

It is a number of years ago now that I received a telephone call asking me to prayerfully consider becoming a trustee of the charity. I count it as a gift from God that I felt very sure of His encouragement for me to take up the role. It opened up opportunities for me to meet so many wonderful men and women of God leading fellowships and churches throughout Israel as well as getting to know needy families within those congregations who are assisted and supported by the charity. I have met single parent families, very needy families, women who are in difficult marriages, addicts and ex-prisoners, all of whom are being helped by regular support from the Mount Moriah Trust. The work is expanding year on year, and Kathy and Tony are completely hands-on as founders and Trustees, being in regular personal contact with the network of pastors supported by the Trust, as well as arranging for all the financial provision to get to where it is needed. One other important aspect of the Mount Moriah Trust that I find so honourable is that one hundred percent of the charity's income goes to those in need.

That evening back in 2007 at the Dan Panorama Hotel when I met Kathy and Tony was an evening that was to have such an impact on me. Almost every year I look forward with such anticipation and excitement to seeing those Pastors, their families and congregations that I have got to know in Israel because I went along with a friend to meet someone she had helped. The Lord has plans and purposes for us, His Word says, plans to prosper us and not to harm us, plans for our future. He certainly had a plan for me that evening, for which I will always thank Him; a plan to become involved with the Mount Moriah Trust's work to support those in need in the land of Israel.

Tony & Sally Tester in Chippenham, UK

As Christians we owe so much to the Jews. Jesus our Saviour was Jewish (John 4:22), for He is King of the Jews (John 19:21). The Bible we so treasure is a Jewish book written by Jewish writers under the inspiration of the Holy Ghost. The early church (the Ecclesia) was predominantly Jewish. Theirs were the adoption, the glory, the covenants, the giving of the Law, the service of God, the promises and the Fathers... the Patriarchs (Romans 9:4–5). It is by the grace of God alone we have been grafted into the 'Commonwealth of Israel' and are partakers of the root and fatness of the olive tree (Ephesians 2:12, and Romans 11:17). Therefore, we have nothing to boast of (Romans 11:18–19), but to recognise the Hebraicness of our faith.

Therefore, we owe the Jews a great debt; our salvation, our future hope, our all has come through our Hebraic roots (Romans 11:17); and as we share in their spiritual blessings, it is our duty to minister to them out of our material blessings (Romans 15:27); to provoke them to jealousy (Romans 11:11), and to pray ultimately for their salvation (Romans 11:25–27).

This is why it is a privilege to support the work that God is doing through the Mount Moriah Trust, as God's humble servants, Tony and Kathy Stewart facilitate the work and make it possible; where such would not be possible for most individual believers, to have a good knowledge and working relationship with Messianic congregations and ministries within the land of Israel. Tony and Kathy quietly get on with God's work behind the scenes without fuss and fanfare. To God be all the praise and all the glory; and we thank God for this privilege. Amen.

Our first relation with Mount Moriah Trust dated back to the 1990s when a group of us who pray regularly for Israel decided to make a collection to bless the Messianic believers in the Land. I was the treasurer and had the joy of seeing God's blessing flowing from our nation to Israel. The symbol of MMT is itself very interesting and testifies to the fact that God is the Provider, be it at the time of Abraham's sacrifice of Isaac at Mount Moriah or at the time of having only a basket of five loaves and two fish that were yet more than enough for more than 5,000 men in need during Jesus' times. Today, we serve the same God who is our Jehovah Jireh, the same God of Abraham, Isaac, and Jacob who provides!

Brian and Brenda Baldwin in Mortimer Common, UK

We first heard of the Mount Moriah Trust through Ruth Drinkwater (now Evans), a very faithful supporter of Prayer for Israel and of the Lord's work in that country.

Since then, we have had the opportunity to travel to Israel twice with a Christian group. On one trip we were privileged to meet members of the amazing church at Cana in Galilee, several Israeli followers of Yeshua, and a number of Ethiopian Christians, all of whom had extraordinary stories to tell. Our son and family were SIM (Serving In Mission) missionaries in Ethiopia and, over the course of our visits to them, we fell in love with the country and its people. So it was lovely to meet Pastor Tal and Tigi in Israel and to be wowed by their faith and commitment.

Nethanel & Tabitha Lam in Singapore

It is amazing how God still remembers our connection with Mount Moriah Trust and more so the needs of His people in Israel! By His grace, we were introduced to Tony & Kathy by a dear common friend who lives in Israel and whom we came to know through our prayer group's giving!

We first met Tony & Kathy during their trip to Singapore in 2013. We soon understood that they took time to visit supporters of MMT and to continue to trust God to expand the ministry for His people. They also took time to be in Israel for a few months every year to be with the local Messianic & Arab congregations, pastors, and leaders, to carefully ascertain their needs so that the resources were appropriately distributed. All these travels of Tony & Kathy were purely on their own expense so that worldwide supporters' contributions went directly to their intended purpose.

We are thankful to the God of Israel for raising Tony & Kathy for MMT and the team that is working with them in the ministry. We are also thankful to the many believers in Singapore who share the same passion for blessing the people of God in the Land through MMT. For many who do not have the chance to be on the grounds with the local congregations, it is comforting to know that their financial supports are reaching the hearts of the believers in Israel through MMT.

We thank our heavenly Father for indeed it is He who supplies seed to the sower and bread for food. He will continue to supply and increase the store of seed in MMT to enlarge the harvest of righteousness in the Land! We also want to thank God for making us rich in every way so that we can be generous on every occasion, and through MMT, through Tony & Kathy, our generosity will result in thanksgiving to God!

We want to give honour where honour is due by testifying that Tony & Kathy are indeed a marvellous couple, full of faith and might, never lacking in their service and works unto the LORD. Their love for the brethren in Israel, and their faithfulness to the call in MMT are an excellent example for many in the Kingdom of God. They have a good legacy; we will continually remember their work produced by faith, their labour prompted by love, and their endurance inspired by hope in our Lord Jesus Christ! We are thankful for their sincere friendship and fellowship with us each time they were in Singapore. We have enjoyed every moment with them and were always blessed more than we ever ask or imagine!

God's Word is our foundation and MMT is the manifestation of God's grace and truth to His people in the Land!

The King will reply, "I tell you the truth, whatever you did for one of the least of these brothers of mine, you did for me." Matthew 25:40

Therefore, as we have opportunity, let us do good to all people, especially to those who belong to the family of believers. Galatians 6:10

Religion that God our Father accepts as pure and faultless is this: to look after orphans and widows in their distress and to keep oneself from being polluted by the world. James 1:27

Gwenda Kuo, Singapore

2013 was the beginning of my spiritual journey where the Lord started to reveal to me about Israel and His heart for His people through various ministries. It was a new season of learning to follow the prompting of the Holy Spirit. I started attending teaching on the book of Revelation, attended seminars on the Hebrew roots of end times prophecy, Purim and Christ in the Passover. A friend sent me an email regarding your meeting at the Bible House and I felt led to attend. While I was there listening to your presentation, I started becoming tearful and sensed I had to respond. Hence, I went forward to speak briefly with you to find out more. I shared with James, my husband about MMT's work in Israel through watching your DVD and so this began our journey in supporting believers in Israel through MMT.

Wayne & Pauline Perry in Batemans Bay, NSW, Australia

We support Israel because if God is for them, how could we be against them. Supporting MMT has meant that we can affirm our support for God's chosen people in a prayerful and practical way.

Before moving to Batemans Bay we lived in Ballina, NSW and providentially, we had been attending a "support Israel" prayer and praise group each month and when Tony & Kathy came and spoke to the Ballina Church Fellowship we had a real peace about supporting the MMT.

This is not to say that we don't support other causes but the Bible tells us "*to do good to all men especially those of the household of faith* (both Jew and Gentile)."

Chapter 29

Join the Lord in His Work

*Now, however, I am on my way to Jerusalem in the service
of the Lord's people there. For Macedonia and Achaia were
pleased to make a contribution for the poor among the
Lord's people in Jerusalem. They were pleased to do it, and
indeed they owe it to them. For if the Gentiles have shared in
the Jews' spiritual blessings, they owe it to the Jews to share
with them their material blessings.*
Romans 15:25-27

Little has changed in over 2,000 years for the believers in Christ in
the Holy Land. They are still being persecuted and harassed and, just
as Apostle Paul said, they need the help of believers outside the Holy
Land to survive, prosper and grow.

If, whilst reading this book, the Lord has touched your heart to join
Him in His work to help the Body of Christ in the Holy Land please
contact us using the details below or visit the Mount Moriah Trust
website where you can subscribe to our news and prayer letters or
make a donation: www.mountmoriah.org.uk

Tony and I would be delighted to discuss a visit to your church or
prayer group, whatever country you live in. Please get in touch with
us using the details below:

The Mount Moriah Trust
P.O.Box 1229
Sandhurst
GU47 7EU
United Kingdom
Tel: +44 (0)1252 879 388
E-Mail: mount.moriah@btinternet.com
www.mountmoriah.org.uk

Let it be known that

Kathy And Tony

ascended to the skies in a

Virgin Hot Air Balloon

on *5ᵗʰ September 2006*

The above is certified by

Pilot in Command

Congratulations!

Virgin Balloon Flight Certificate. (Chapter 7)

Certificate
of Appreciation

Kathy & Tony Stewart

On the occasion of your visit I am honored to recognize you as a true friend of Israel. Your arrival at this particular moment in our history is an expression of support and solidarity that is deeply appreciated.

I am honored to name you as an Ambassador of Goodwill for Israel.

I trust that you have enjoyed and been inspired by your visit and that it has served to strengthen your bonds with the people and State of Israel. I know that you will encourage further tourism to the Holy Land by sharing your meaningful experiences with friends, family and community.

We look forward to welcoming you again here soon.

**Benyamin Elon
Minister of Tourism**

MINISTRY OF TOURISM

Jerusalem 2003

Certificate of Appreciation from the Minister of Tourism thanking us for our visit in 2003 when tourism was almost non-existent because of the Intifada. (Chapter 15)

My Grandfather Staff Sergeant George Greig who died near Jaffa shortly before the end of WW1 on 18ᵗʰ October 1918.

His grave in the Commonwealth War Graves Commission Cemetery in Ramleh, Israel. (Chapter 25)

*Ken Burnett
Founder of Prayer
For Israel and
first Patron of the
Mount Moriah
Trust. (Chapter 12)*

*Meeting with David Hathaway in Tel Aviv in 2015.
From left to right: Tony, David, Kathy, Katie Morris (David's PA)
(Chapter 18)*

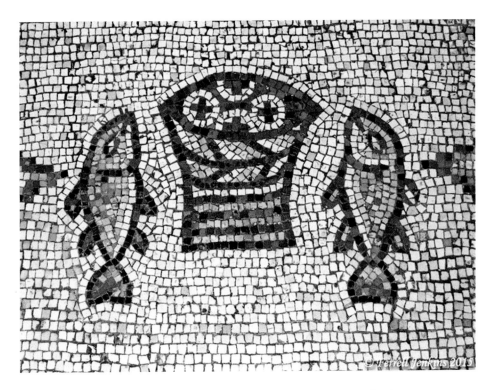

Mosaic of the loaves and fishes in the Church of the Multiplication at Tabgha on the western shore of the Sea of Galilee where Jesus fed the 5,000. The inspiration for the Mount Moriah Trust logo below. (Chapter 15)

Pat Ramsay co-founder of Shalom Israel in Melbourne, Australia (Chapter 21)

Brothers and Sisters in Christ. Celebrating Pat Ramsay's 80th Birthday in February 2019 From left to right: Tony, Kathy, Phil and Pat Ramsay

New beds provided for Pastor Tal Shiferaw's children and the broken window mended. (Chapter 15)

Pastor Tal Shiferaw delivering food parcels to the needy in his Kehilat Beit El congregation in Jerusalem. (Chapter 15)

The end of morning "Devotions" at the House of Hope in Bethlehem (Chapter 17)

Blind men in the House of Hope making brooms. (Chapter 17)

Pastor Dov Bikas and Pastor Eduard Bitiev set off on their "Coca-Cola Ministry" to the drug and alcohol addicts around the old bus station in southern Tel Aviv. (Chapter 17)

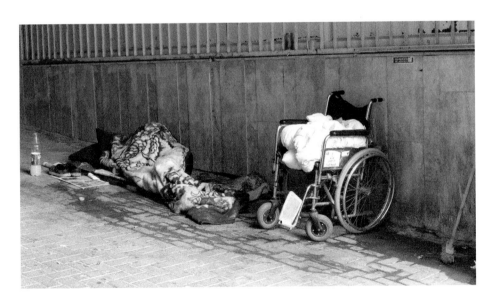

A homeless person living on the street in Jerusalem in 2015.

Pastor Munir Kakish, staff and boys at the Home of New life in Ramallah (Chapter 17)

A local farmer brings the Home of New Life the gift of a sheep to provide them with meat. (Chapter 17)

Elmira Brodkin giving the Gospel message to those attending the Grace House soup kitchen in Beersheva. (Chapter 17)

Children enjoying the Cana Baptist Church Children's Bible Camp. (Chapter 16)

Children from Pastor Zechariah Arni's Retzon Ha'El congregation enjoying a day out at a theme park funded by the Trust as a special summer holiday treat.

Pastor Zechariah Arni loading his car with food parcels to be delivered to poor Ethiopian believers in the Retzon Ha'El congregation in Haifa. (Chapter 17)

At the House of Light Tony and Anis Barhoum are loading mattresses onto the van before setting off to distribute food and other essentials to needy families.

Kathy, Anis and Nawal Barhoum unloading food, blankets and mattresses to help single mother Amira (right) who has six sons, cope with the cold winter nights in a bare and shabby apartment with little heating. (Chapter 16)

Aaron and Hur holding up Moses hands. This is the carving on the top of the central pillar of the Menorah that stands outside the Knesset. The British Government presented the Menorah to Israel in 1956 in honour of the eighth Anniversary of Israel's Independence. (Chapter 22)

Bibliography

Chapter 4
The Road to Carmel   David Davis

Chapter 9
Streams in the Desert L. B. Cowman
The God Chasers   Tommy Tenney
Elijah – Anointed and Stressed Jeff Lucas
The Elijah Legacy   David Davis
Encouraging Women Priscilla Reid

Chapter 13
A People Tall and Smooth Judith Galblum Pex